THE RUSSIAN FAR EAST

Strategic Development of the Workforce

THE RUSSIAN FAR EAST

Strategic Development of the Workforce

IRINA V. NOVIKOVA

Editorial Research Supervisors

Sergey M. Darkin and Vladimir L. Kvint

To Stanford Libraries,
Prof. V. Kvint

AAP | APPLE
ACADEMIC
PRESS

NYC
2024
april 12

First edition published [2021]

Apple Academic Press Inc.
1265 Goldenrod Circle, NE,
Palm Bay, FL 32905 USA

4164 Lakeshore Road, Burlington,
ON, L7L 1A4 Canada

CRC Press
6000 Broken Sound Parkway NW,
Suite 300, Boca Raton, FL 33487-2742 USA

2 Park Square, Milton Park,
Abingdon, Oxon, OX14 4RN UK

© 2021 Apple Academic Press, Inc.

Apple Academic Press exclusively co-publishes with CRC Press, an imprint of Taylor & Francis Group, LLC

Library and Archives Canada Cataloguing in Publication

Title: The Russian Far East : strategic development of the workforce / Irina V. Novikova ; editorial research supervisors, Sergey M. Darkin and Vladimir L. Kvint.

Names: Novikova, I. V. (Irina Viktorovna), author.

Description: Includes bibliographical references and index.

Identifiers: Canadiana (print) 20200298674 | Canadiana (ebook) 20200298895 | ISBN 9781774630013 (softcover) | ISBN 9781774630006 (hardcover) | ISBN 9781003132158 (ebook)

Subjects: LCSH: Labor supply—Russia (Federation)—Russian Far East. | LCSH: Labor market—Russia (Federation)—Russian Far East. | LCSH: Manpower policy—Russia (Federation)—Russian Far East.

Classification: LCC HD5797.2.F27 N68 2021 | DDC 331.12/04209474—dc23

Library of Congress Cataloging-in-Publication Data

Names: Novikova, I. V. (Irina Viktorovna) author.

Title: The Russian Far East : strategic development of the workforce / Irina V. Novikova.

Description: 1st Edition. | Palm Bay : Apple Academic Press, 2020. | Includes bibliographical references and index. | Summary: "This monograph The Russian Far East: Strategic Development of the Workforce by Irina V. Novikova presents an integrated concept of the workforce development strategy for the Far Eastern Federal District (FEFD) of Russia. This concept is based on the strategizing methodology developed by Vladimir L. Kvint. The concept takes into account contemporary global, national, and regional development trends in workforce, employment, and labor market issues, including the active influence of information and communication technologies (ICT) and the appearance of numerous novel forms of employment"-- Provided by publisher.

Identifiers: LCCN 2020034719 (print) | LCCN 2020034720 (ebook) | ISBN 9781774630006 (hardcover) | ISBN 9781003132158 (ebook)

Subjects: LCSH: Manpower policy--Russia (Federation)--Russian Far East. | Russian Far East (Russia)--Economic conditions. | Russian Far East (Russia)--Economic policy. | Information technology--Russia (Federation)--Russian Far East.

Classification: LCC HD5797.F37 N68 2020 (print) | LCC HD5797.F37 (ebook) | DDC 331.12/04209577--dc23

LC record available at https://lccn.loc.gov/2020034719
LC ebook record available at https://lccn.loc.gov/2020034720

ISBN: 978-1-77463-000-6 (hbk)
ISBN: 978-1-77463-001-3 (pbk)
ISBN: 978-1-003-13215-8 (ebk)

About the Author

IRINA V. NOVIKOVA, DSc

Irina V. Novikova, Dr. Sc. (Economics), is Professor at the Economic and Financial Strategy Department at Lomonosov Moscow State University's Moscow School of Economics and a leading researcher at the Center for Strategic Studies at the Institute of Mathematical Research of Complex Systems under Lomonosov Moscow State University.

For more than twenty years she has been studying the formation and development of labor resources, employment, unemployment, and the labor market. She has more than 120 published research papers within this scientific field. She is a developer of corporate and regional strategies for the improvement of labor resources, employment, and improving quality of life.

About the Editorial Research Supervisors

Sergey M. Darkin, PhD

Sergey Darkin, PhD, was the Governor of the Primorsky Region of the Russian Federation from 2001 to 2012, Deputy Minister of Regional Development of the Russian Federation from 2012 to 2014, and is currently President of the Pacific Investment Group (TIGR) since 2014. Dr. Darkin currently serves as a board member of several leading companies and banks. He is an authority in issues of Asia-Pacific economic development and a well-established professional in regional cooperation and the shipping and fishing industries, among other areas.

Dr. Vladimir Kvint, Sc. (Economics)

Dr. Vladimir Kvint, Sc. (Economics), has been Professor of Strategy, Management Systems and International Economics at Fordham University, New York University's Stern School of Business, American and LaSalle Universities, and Babson College and serves as Chair of the Economic and Financial Strategy Department in the Moscow School of Economics at Lomonosov Moscow State University. He is also Research Director at the Center for Strategic Studies at the Institute of Complex Systems Mathematical Research (CSS ICSMR). Dr. Kvint is a member of the Bretton Woods Committee, a Life Time Foreign Member of the Russian Academy of Science, a U. S. Fulbright Scholar, and a well-established strategic advisor.

Contents

Abbreviations

ADTs	advanced development territories
AI	artificial intelligence
ASEDT	advanced social and economic development territories
CIS	commonwealth of independent states
CPSU	Communist Party of the Soviet Union
EDC	employee's digital competence
FEFD	Far Eastern Federal District
GEL	global economic linkages
HCDA	Human Capital Development Agency
ICT	information and communication technologies
IILS	International Institute for Labor Studies
R&D	research and development
SME	small and medium enterprises
WDCs	workplace digital components
DPE	digital potential of employment

About the Book

This monograph *The Russian Far East: Strategic Development of the Workforce* by Irina V. Novikova presents an integrated concept of the workforce development strategy for the Far Eastern Federal District (FEFD) of Russia. This concept is based on the strategizing methodology developed by Vladimir L. Kvint. The concept takes into account contemporary global, national, and regional development trends in workforce, employment, and labor market issues, including the active influence of information and communication technologies (ICT) and the appearance of numerous novel forms of employment.

The conclusions and proposals in this work are built on the analysis of a wide range of analytical data. Workforce development programs, from the Tsarist era until the present, are analyzed in this work. Here, creative approaches to the workforce provision problems of the Russian Far East and appraisal criteria for the strategy's public and economic efficiency are proposed.

This work is of interest to a wide range of experts, researchers, and employees of government agencies who are concerned with the issues of strategic workforce development in the Russian Far Eastern Federal District. In addition, this study will benefit those who reside in the region, and those who intend to relocate to, reside, and work in the area of the Russian Far East. This book belongs to the Strategy of the Russian Far East Library developed under the editorial supervision of Sergey Darkin and Vladimir Kvint.

Introduction

The Far Eastern Federal District (FEFD) is an amazingly beautiful and rich region that is a part of Russia due to tremendous human efforts, lots of lost lives, and ruined fates. This is not only a vast territory (36% of the country's total area) with a variety of natural and climatic zones, minerals, and precious metals; the region is also home to residents who share an unmatched mentality and culture. Natives of the Russian Far East are unique people—they are cheerful, friendly, and hospitable, despite the daily challenges they face. As the region is remote and to a certain extent isolated from the country's center and central government, the residents of the region are somewhat detached from the rest of the nation and are used to solving problems on their own, as it is not always possible to get help from outside. Therefore, all issues are dealt with according to internal and regional rules and traditions. Anything that comes from the center (i.e., inspections and auditors) is perceived by many inhabitants of the Russian Far East as interference that they just need to live through. For after it is over, they will be able to live as quietly as before those visits (i.e., by their own codes and rules). The Russian Far East is still hard to reach by transport. It takes at least seven hours to fly from Moscow to Khabarovsk or to Vladivostok by plane. This is enough time for Far Easterners to "erect their Potemkin villages."

Far Easterners are hard-workers. They are quite industrious and enterprising. Despite their mostly European origins, the residents of the region are quite well adapted to communicate with the Asian aboriginal population and understand the nature and temper of those residents.

The entire population of the Russian Far East can be roughly classified according to the following three groups:

- Those who dream of leaving the region and may do so at some point in the future;
- Those who would like to leave the region, but are not currently able and will not be able to in the future; and
- Those who love the Russian Far East and view it as the only place they would ever live.

The first two groups behave like "time servers" who use the region's resources and have no interest in developing it. The prosperity of the Russian Far East is based only on outcomes of the activity of the third group, who view it as their true home and homeland. It is also worth noting here that a major portion of the region borders with densely populated and rapidly developing countries.

No "time server" will protect this land. Therefore, any proposals to develop the Russian Far East using rotational team methods are, in our opinion, not just utopian, but even treasonous.

The second factor that appears to be the main impediment to the region's development today is the weak social orientation of all development programs in the Russian Far East. Today, the development of education, healthcare, and culture are underestimated or in some cases ignored altogether. For instance, the *Russian Far East In-Demand Occupations Guide for 2018–2025* prepared by the Human Capital Development Agency (HCDA) in the Russian Far East lists the following key sectors in the region: coal, ore, and gold mining, construction, machinery manufacturing, fisheries, and aquafarming, agriculture, and food industry, wood industry, transportation, and logistics, tourism, and consumer services. Thus, the region is mainly viewed as the country's natural resource base, with the development of the social sphere (i.e., culture, arts, science, education, and sports) not being a priority at present. The development of the region's social and cultural needs is not on the agenda today. This vision of the region's development as a rightful constituent of the Russian Federation is not a forward-thinking one. Developers of programs for the Russian Far East should understand that the region is home to people with the same cultural and social needs as all other citizens of Russia, who want to live as a whole family, raise kids, go to theaters, do sports, etc. It has been a long time since the Russian Far East was a place for forced labor camps and a colony for exiled offenders—today it is a region of decent people who want to live a decent life. Without understanding such seemingly simple things, no program will work and the region will see no development. In the worst-case scenario, the area will be taken over by other nations. In fact, many of the numerous initiatives that are being implemented now in the Russian Far East seem designed to meet the interests of other nations, rather than those of the local population.

The city of Vladivostok—the center of the Russian Far East—is Russia's cultural, educational, scientific, and economic face directed toward the countries of the Asia Pacific region. The concept of turning the capital of Primorye (the coastland) into a key city in Northeast Asia was proposed back in 1993 by V. M. Mikhailov, a Far Eastern researcher. He suggested that "Vladivostok in the Pacific must become an international center similar to Geneva in Europe." (Geneva is the home city of the UN's European Office.)[1]

The 2012 APEC summit held in Vladivostok showed that the city and the region do have this opportunity. Developing the city to a global level will be a powerful growth point for the Russian Far East and the country at large. This book provides a new view of the potential for the development of the Far East, which is in keeping with

---

1. Mikhailov, V., (1993). *Vladivostok May Become an International Center of Asia Pacific Region*. Vladivostok.

today's conditions, and taking into account the global trends and the use of cutting-edge technologies. In this book, the Russian Far East is viewed as being an area where every resident can pursue a decent life and living. The author is convinced that only on this condition can we expect the region to enjoy efficient full-scale development.

Preface

TO READERS OF THE STRATEGY OF THE RUSSIAN FAR EAST LIBRARY

In many regions of the world, the population is not only a workforce as a factor of extended reproduction; it is a symbol and a factor of integration into the history of global civilization. Such a perception of labor potential mainly concerns new development areas and under-populated areas. Among such regions is the Far East of Russia, the largest country in the world.

With the high level of natural resource development in the European part of the Russian Federation, a significant part of the colossal natural wealth of the Russian Far East is still in its initial period of involvement in the economic turnover of this country and, in addition, of the global economy.

The population of the Russian Far East, besides its role in the development of natural resources and productive power in the region, plays a prominent role in ensuring its Russian identity, security, and finally, its undisputable belonging to Russia. Nevertheless, the principal economical function of the Russian Far East residents is their role as the most important factor of economic prosperity in both the region and Russia as a whole. It is the economic power of the population—its role as the workforce—that Irina V. Novikova's book *The Russian Far East: Strategic Development of the Workforce* deals with. Throughout her academic career, the author has been studying the labor resources of the Russian Far East, the region in which she was born, grew up, and became a researcher.

This book does not begin directly with an analysis of the region's labor resources but studies the complicated economic life of the Russian Far East since the very first efforts back in the Tsarist era to settle and open up the region. It is just as important that the author considers all known strategic developments and approaches of these past periods of development in the Russian Far East—one of the largest regions of Russia. In particular, the author investigates practically all of the long-term programs of both the Soviet epoch ("Siberia" and "Far East") and of the new Russia. It is important to stress that in the second chapter the author sets forth her strategic vision of workforce development trends and dynamics in the Far Eastern Federal District (FEFD) for the period from 2005 to 2018.

In the third chapter, Professor Novikova defines factors of motivation for the region's workforce. In the fourth chapter, the author builds on this research to outline the main conceptual elements of the FEFD's workforce development strategy until 2035, which is aimed at full and high-quality development of the region's human potential.

Novikova's book contributes greatly to the study and substantiation of strategic prospects for the development of the Russian Far East. Therefore, with this monograph, we continue to add important publications to the Strategy of the Russian Far East Library we launched in 2015.

—Sergey Darkin, PhD
Vladimir Kvint, PhD

CHAPTER 1 | Analysis of Key Practices for the Development of the Russian Far East's Labor Resources

1.1 LABOR RESOURCE ENDOWMENT IN THE RUSSIAN FAR EAST DURING THE TSAR PERIOD

The development of the Russian Far East was associated with the need to capture and hold this region within its borders. These territories were claimed by powerful neighbors: China, Japan, Korea, and the USA. The colonization of the Russian Far East began for purposes other than the economic development of the territory. The initial objective of the Tsarist government in the Russian Far East was to hold the country's outlying region and improve its defense potential.[1] By the early 1860s, the population of the Russian Far East was 352.5 thousand in the region of Zabaikalskaya, 13.9 thousand in the Amur, and 35.1 thousand in Primorskaya. The aboriginal population was scarce in number and indifferent to Russian allegiance. According to 1897 population census data, the aboriginal population totaled 17.9 thousand.[2] By the beginning of the twentieth century, the population decreased and, in 1916, amounted to 15.9 thousand (3% of the total population of the Russian Far East).[3] Therefore, it was the Russian population that the authorities were interested in relocating to the Russian Far East to settle the colonized territories. Numerous decrees were adopted that

---

1. Kolosovskiy, N. N., Lagutin, A. N., & Tselishchev, M. I., (1926). *Economy of the Russian Far East: Collection* (p. 314). Moscow: Planovoye Khozyaistvo.

2. Alexeyev, A. I., & Morozov, B. N., (1989). *Development of the Russian Far East (End of the Nineteenth Century to 1917)* (p. 12). Moscow: Nauka.

3. Kabuzan, V. M., (1976). *How the Russian Far East was Settled* (p. 195). Khabarovsk.

were to contribute to the settlement of the region. The main principles of voluntary and preferential relocation with the right to purchase land were set by the Russian government in the following documents: "Rules for Voluntary Resettlement to Priamurskiy Territory" (1858); "Rules for Settlement of Russians and Foreigners in the Amur and Primorskaya Regions" (1861); and "Decree of Senate Dated April 24, 1861, on Resettlement to the Far East." These laws underlined the necessity of resettlement by whole communities that should unite at least 15 peasant families.[4] Thus, methods of social structure formation in the Far Eastern territory were first defined during this time and peasants became the prevailing part of that population.

It must be noted that, at this time, the region had no elementary infrastructure and severe climatic conditions, without adequate living conditions. This was the basis of attracting peasants who, being in dire straits, made their decision to migrate and settle in this harsh land. Even the road to the Russian Far East was very long and difficult. There were many who had to cancel their decision to migrate and stopped while on the way to Far Eastern borders. Some died on their months-long journey. Migration in large groups, consisting of 15 or more families, was a strategic and correct decision. Such communities were quicker to adapt and settle down, and they developed their settlements on the basis of mutual support.

The basis of "Rules for Settlement of Russians and Foreigners in the Amur and Primorskaya Regions" were principles of voluntary and concessional migration allowing the right to acquire ownership of land. The rules directed the following:

1. All who wished to settle in the Amur and Primorskaya regions were to be allotted unoccupied plots of crown lands for temporary possession or for absolute legal ownership;

---

4. Busse, F. F., (1896). *In-Migration of Peasants by Sea to Yuzhno-Ussuriyskiy Territory in 1883–1893* (p. 32). St. Petersburg.

2. All who wished to settle in a community consisting of at least 15 families should be allotted a continuous land plot provided that each family received not more than 100 *dessiatines* (2700 acres);

3. Within the territory from the headwaters of the Ussuri River and downstream to the sea such land plots were to be allotted to the whole peasant community for use in perpetuity and on a permanent basis. A peasant community was entitled to sell a land plot to any other peasant community consisting of at least fifteen families;

4. In all other localities, land plots allotted to peasant communities were to be freely leased for use for 20 years, but peasant localities were neither to sell nor dispose of such land plots.

Significant benefits to resettlers were provided by the Edict of the Russian Senate, dated April 24, 1861. Pursuant to the tenth paragraph of the Edict, all resettlers who migrated to the Far East at their own expense were relieved from recruiting duty for 10 recruitment campaign terms; in addition, they were released forever from payment of a head tax, and were to pay the land tax only on expiration of twenty years (from the date of the edict).

Throughout all the stages of economic development in the Russian East, resettlement policy was aimed at increasing the economically active Russian farming population in order to fully meet the food requirements of the region. It is necessary to note that the natural and geographical location of the region corresponds to agricultural risk, with negative manifestations gradually increasing from the south to the north. However, food security and independence in the Far Eastern territories was quite correctly considered by the Russian state as the development priority of this region.

Since the development of the region was agrarian, the "Rules" determined the procedure of mostly voluntary massive peasant resettlements. In 1861, "Temporary Rules for Resettlement of Peasants to

Crown Lands" were published. In one year, new "Rules for Resettlement of Peasants at Their Own Expense" were adopted that stimulated resettlement at peasants' own cost.[5] These two documents were the first efforts to formulate fundamental state policy objectives concerning the resettlement problem whose focus was the independence and economic activity of peasants. The most effective policies were family resettlements, since families had natural reproductive potential and, to a lesser extent, were prone to migration mobility.

Among governmental decisions concerning the organization of the mass resettlement program and adopted at the beginning of the twentieth century, one should note "Provisional Rules on Voluntary Resettlement of Rural Residents and Petty Landowners" of 1904. These "provisional rules" contained "the government's expectations concerning the solution of the social strain occurring in Russia's central regions." It was supposed to relocate so-called "insecure persons" to the frontier regions.

Since beginning from the 1890s land-poor and landless peasants who were unable to pay traveling expenses made up the majority of resettlers, in 1893 a new reduced resettlement tariff was introduced equal to one-third of the travel charge in Class 4 railway cars. In addition, resettlers were provided with mileage allowance, medical care, and food products, although in insufficient amounts. Installation loans did not exceed 150 rubles per family in Primorye and 100 rubles in all other resettlement regions. The settlement money was granted by installments, with great delays, while economists calculated that at least 450 rubles were needed by a resettler to relocate and for start-up expenses.

Upon arrival in the Far East, all new settlers could get a 100 dessiatine land plot per family; they were relieved from all arrears and, in addition, were granted a five-year relief from all government charges.

---

5. Busse, F. F., (1896). *In-Migration of Peasants by Sea to Yuzhno-Ussuriyskiy Territory in 1883–1893* (pp. 53, 57). St. Petersburg.

The government also provided support to purchase farm equipment. Nevertheless, permits to resettle to Amur or to Primorskaya regions were provided only to comparatively prosperous peasants, as the authorities demanded that each family was to bring along at least 600 rubles, and could procure all necessary things at their arrival.

At the beginning of the twentieth century, the situation began to change. On June 22, 1900, new "temporary rules" for the formation of resettlement plots in the Amur and Primorskaya regions were approved. According to these rules, starting from January 1, 1901, instead of a 100 dessiatines family plot, resettlers received no more than 15 dessiatines (16.35 ha) of arable land per male family member, including a forest area. Nevertheless, settlements formed before January 1, 1901, and not receiving land allotment were provided with land at the former rate. Amur River region and Primorye region were settled by self-supporting settlers.

Since June 5, 1904, the Russian Far East was already being developed according to the decree "On Resettlement to Crown Lands" that was extended to all regions. However, Stolypin's reform finally liquidated the special, preferential status of the Russian Far East region as a leading colonized region of the country. Migration to frontier regions became perhaps a fundamental principle of the Tsarist regime's policy, but many of the border lands (such as Western Siberia and the steppe zone) had in this respect a much more favorable geographic position than the Far Eastern Region. This region, deprived of its main advantages and attractive power, began ceding ground.

Thus, the *main goals of Tsarist Russia were the settlement of Far Eastern territories and the formation of an established, robust population, notwithstanding the negative economic effects of numerous implemented measures. The territory of the Far East was to be colonized by the Russian population, which was ready to finally settle on it. The result was a dramatic increase in population, and of rural and urban settlements.* One of the weaknesses of the Tsarist government's policy in the

Russian Far East was no support for the population already residing in the territory, and that created a certain social strain and the rejection of resettlers who had significant benefits. Besides, when the grace period and government subsidies ended, many resettlers would leave the Far Eastern Region.

1.2 SOVIET MECHANISMS TO STRENGTHEN THE ATTRACTIVENESS OF EMPLOYMENT IN THE REGION

In the Soviet period, objectives of settlement in the Far Eastern Region changed, although its protective function remained. The Russian Far East for the first time was viewed as a locality where people already lived, whose permanent home had complicated environmental and economic conditions. A decree was then developed to improve the living standards of the local population. The decree of the USSR Council of Ministers, dated August 1946, and named "On the Increase of Wages and Construction of Dwellings for Workers, Technicians, and Engineers Employed at Enterprises and Construction Projects Located in the Urals, Siberia, and the Far East" provided the following measures:

"Taking into account that severe climatic conditions of the territories of the Urals, Siberia, and the Far East create additional difficulties for workers, technicians, and engineers engaged in hard work—during mining of coal, minerals, oil, and in the metal industry, construction, and cargo-handling operations—the USSR Council of Ministers finds it necessary to:

- Increase, against existing rates, wages for the above categories of workers, technicians, and engineers, and;
- Considerably expand the program of residential construction in the Urals, Siberia, and the Far East for workers, technicians, and engineers engaged in heavy manual operations. For this purpose, the USSR Council of Ministers decrees that:

1. From September 1, 1946, in the Urals, Siberia, and Far East wages shall be increased by 20% for: workers, technicians, and engineers of collieries directly engaged in mining and load-handling operations; workers, technicians, and engineers of ironworks and non-ferrous smelters directly engaged at hot workshops, mines, and during load-handling operations; workers, technicians, and engineers of oil industry enterprises directly engaged in oil production and drilling operations; workers, technicians, and engineers engaged in production of peat, graphite, mica, asbestos, and cement manufacturing, as well as in salt production; workers, technicians, and engineers in the chemical industry directly engaged in unhealthy and hot work, in mines and in loading and unloading operations; workers, technicians, and engineers in the ministry's construction projects; in heavy industry, fuel handling, military, and naval industries, iron, and steel industry enterprises, and the oil industry in the eastern regions of the USSR; and in non-ferrous and chemical industries directly engaged in construction and assembly operations.

2. Set that wage increase specified in paragraph one of this Decree extends to 824,000 workers, technicians, and engineers engaged at 727 enterprises and construction works in the Urals, Siberia, and the Far East according to the list approved by the USSR Council of Ministers. In order to increase wages for the above categories of workers, technicians, and engineers, the relevant ministries shall increase the annual wage and salaries fund by 1,400 million rubles.

3. Approve the following residential construction program in the districts of the Urals, Siberia, and the Far East to be completed within H2 1946 and 1947: in total 60,750 residential houses with a total floor area of 4,200 thousand

square meters, including: 50,650 single-family residential houses consisting of two or three rooms with a kitchen (wooden or stone); 10,100 communal residential houses (wooden or stone) with 55,000 apartments.

4. Stipulate that 50,650 single-family residential houses are to be built in H2 1946 and in 1947 shall be sold to workers, technicians, engineers, and office employees at the following price: log house (with two rooms and a kitchen)—8 thousand rubles; stone house (with two rooms and a kitchen)—10 thousand rubles; log house (with three rooms and a kitchen—10 thousand Rubles; stone house (with three rooms and a kitchen)—12 thousand rubles.

5. In order to provide workers, technicians, engineers, and office employees with the opportunity to purchase a residential house, Central Communal Bank must grant 8–10 thousand rubles' loans with 10 years' maturity to individuals who purchase two-room houses, and 10–12 thousand rubles' loans with 12 years' maturity to individuals who purchase two-room houses, with collection of 1% in loan interest per annum.

Oblige the USSR Ministry of Finance to budget up to 1 billion rubles for loans to workers, technicians, engineers, and office employees."

This document both stimulated migration to the Russian Far East and improved living standards of the people who already resided there.

In 1967, the Decree of the USSR Council of Ministers No. 638 named "On Further Measures Aimed at the Development of Productive Forces of the Far Eastern Economic Region and Chita Region" was adopted.

In compliance with the decision of the 23rd Congress of the Communist Party of the Soviet Union (CPSU) and "On Further Measures," and the accelerated drawing into economic circulation of the natural wealth of Primorskiy and Khabarovsk territories, Yakut

ASSR, Amur, Kamchatka, Magadan, Sakhalin, and Chita regions, and in order to improve the living conditions of the population in these regions, the CPSU Central Committee and USSR Council of Ministers decree as follows:

The provision of workers and other employees of enterprises, organizations, and institutions of the Far Eastern economic region and Chita region with additional benefits contributing to personnel retention, the said benefits including: setting a regional pay factor to salaries and wages of workers and office employees for which this pay factor has not yet been set; paying an increased prorated increase in the districts of the Far North and equated localities; gradually reducing state-set retail prices in price area two, and other benefits.

The RSFSR Council of Ministers, Executive Committees of Khabarovsk and Primorskiy territories, Amur, and Chita regions are to organize the proper acceptance of resettlers, ensure their job placements and meet their essential housekeeping needs, build residential houses for resettlers, as a rule, before they arrive at their settlement localities, and timely build kindergartens, nurseries, schools, hospitals, and public utility and catering enterprises.

The RSFSR Council of Ministers, for construction of residential houses for resettlers in Khabarovsk, Amur, and Chita regions, is to allocate capital investments, standard fabricated residential houses, construction, and other materials in amounts that ensure completion of relevant construction schedules.

The USSR State Bank is to ensure the granting of state farms and collective farms in the Khabarovsk and Primorskiy territories, and Amur and Chita regions, according to current-year long-term loan plans, of pre-construction and housing construction loans for resettlers to arrive in the following year.

To establish the following benefits for families that will be relocated to state farms and collective farms in the Khabarovsk and Primorskiy territories, and Amur and Chita regions:

1. Payment of a lump-sum allowance in the amount of 150 rubles per family head and 50 rubles per family member;
2. Issuing an up to 4000 ruble loan for construction of a residential house plus outbuildings, with 50% of the loan principle to be charged to the state budget and the rest of the loan amount to be repaid within fifteen years starting from year five after loan issue;
3. Issuing an up to 400 ruble loan per family for purchase of cow and other cattle, with 50% of the loan principle to be charged to the state budget and the rest loan amount to be repaid within five years starting from year three after loan issue;
4. Providing families resettling to state farms, within a settlement year, with detached houses or apartments, with household plots and haylands of the established area, and exempt them from rental payment, and provide them with fuel and other communal services for free at the standard rates within two years on settlement;
5. Selling, with the consent of the state farm directors, cows out of the reproductive herd at cost, but not higher than the purchase price, and sell within two years after settlement 300 kg of fodder per family holding livestock. Advise collective farms to provide the same benefits to families who settle at collective farms;
6. Exempting settlement localities for ten years the following:

   - Collective farmers and resettlers from agricultural tax;
   - Collective farms enlisting resettlers from income tax by the number of accepted families, and collective farms newly organized by resettlers from payment of the above tax completely;
   - Families relocating to state farms from agricultural tax or income tax collected from the population for farm income.

The USSR State Bank shall collect 0.5% per annum on loans issued to resettlers.

To establish that when sole military members are discharged to the reserve or retire, or other sole individuals resettle to state farms or collective farms of the Khabarovsk and Primorskiy territories, and Amur and Chita regions, the above individuals shall be compensated the cost of travel from the place of discharge or retirement to the place of resettlement and given a lump-sum allowance in the amount of 150 rubles. If the above individuals settle down and start a family within two years from the resettlement date, they shall be provided with benefits (including payment of a lump-sum allowance for family members), as fixed by the Decree for resettlers.

The families arriving to Khabarovsk and Primorskiy territories, and Amur and Chita regions, by invitation to collective and state farms for which a settlement plan was established, provide all benefits stipulated by these Decree for resettlers. Moreover, a lump-sum allowance shall be paid to these families in the amount of 100 rubles per family head and 50 rubles per family member.

In order to further improve living conditions of the population of the Far Eastern economic region and Chita region, to increase the real income of workers and office employees, and to attract and retain personnel, the RSFSR Council of Ministers, ministries, and departments of the USSR shall implement measures aimed at accelerated the construction of residential houses, general education schools, hospitals, and other cultural and public service facilities, as well as the significant improvement of retail trade and development of all public services in these districts.

The State Pricing Committee under the USSR State Planning Committee together with the USSR Ministry of Trade, USSR Ministry of Finance, and RSFSR Council of Ministers are to develop, and submit in 1968 to the USSR Council of Ministers, proposals for a gradual reduction in the Far Eastern Economic Region of state retail prices for vital consumer products (bread, meat, fats, sugar, etc.) down to Price Belt 2 prices.

The USSR State Planning Committee jointly with the State Labor and Wages Committee under the USSR Council of Ministers, the USSR Ministry of Finance, the USSR All-Union Trade Council of Trade Unions and the RSFSR Council of Ministers are within one month developing and submitting to the USSR Council of Ministers the proposals on the procedure and deadlines for the introduction of benefits for employees of the Far Eastern economic region, Chita region, and Buryat ASSR.

Ministries and agencies of the USSR and the RSFSR Council of Ministers are to relocate during 1967 to 1970, subject to established procedure, the necessary number of specialists and qualified workers to newly commissioned enterprises, construction works, and Far Eastern economic region and Chita region organizations.

To commission the Central Committee of the All-Union Leninist Young Communist League jointly with ministries and agencies of the USSR and the RSFSR Council of Ministers to assign annually from 1967–1970 6 to 8 thousand young men and women to be sent to the most important national construction projects and newly commissioned major enterprises of the Far Eastern economic region and Chita region through a public call-up according to Decree No. 441 of the Central Committee of CPSU and the USSR Council of Ministers dated June 6, 1966.

To permit Council of Ministers of Yakut ASSR, Executive Committees of Primorskiy and Khabarovsk Territory Councils of Workers' Deputies, Amur, Kamchatka, Magadan, Sakhalin, and Chita Region Councils of Workers' Deputies to organize workers and office employees, who worked in the regions of the Far North and equated localities for at least fifteen years, into building groups for the construction of residential houses in cities and work settlements of other republics, territories, and regions, except the administrative centers of Union Republics, Moscow, and Leningrad, the Moscow region, and resort localities.

To oblige party and Soviet authorities, heads of enterprises, construction projects, and other organizations to provide every kind of assistance to employees who wish to relocate for permanent residence to the Far Eastern economic region and Chita region.

The USSR Fisheries Ministry will build a 480-bed hospital in Vladivostok from 1967 to 1971, while the USSR Ministry of Maritime Fleet is to build a 240-bed hospital in Primorskiy territory, a 120-bed hospital in Kamchatka region, and an 80-bed hospital in the Sakhalin region from 1967 to 1970.

To accept the proposal of the USSR All-Union Trade Council of Trade Unions to expand current resorts and begin construction of new resorts, rest houses, and tourist centers in the Russian Far East and Chita region according to Annex No. 22.

The USSR Ministry of Higher and Secondary Vocational Education and the RSFSR Council of Ministers jointly with the USSR State Planning Committee and concerned ministries and agencies of the USSR are to decide whether it is expedient to set up from 1971 to 1975 a Polytechnic Institute in Chita, a Technological Institute in Blagoveshchensk, a Forestry Institute in the Khabarovsk (on the basis of the Forest Engineering Faculty of Khabarovsk Polytechnic Institute), a Forestry Faculty of the Primorskiy Agricultural Institute, and an Electric Technical Institute of Communications in the Khabarovsk and submit proposals to the USSR Council of Ministers on this issue.

The Council of Ministers of the RSFSR and the USSR Ministry of Coal Industry, the USSR Ministry of Fishery, the USSR Ministry of Non-ferrous Metallurgy and USSR Ministry for Consumer Goods Industry are to begin from 1967 to 1970 construction of new buildings for educational institutions in the Russian Far East and Chita Region according to Annex No. 23.

The Council of Ministers of the RSFSR and the USSR Ministry of Trade are to improve retail trade services for the population in the Far Eastern economic region and Chita region, increase the number of workplaces by the end of 1970 by up to 51 thousand positions and the number of seats at catering enterprises up to 301.5 thousand seats, increase the storage capacity of general commodity warehouses up to

2,959 thousand square meters, and the storage capacity of vegetable, potato, and fruit storages up to 399.7 thousand tons of maximum storage, with distribution of tasks between territories and regions according to Annex No. 24.

The Council of Ministers of the RSFSR is to develop and implement measures aimed to significantly improve public services, bearing in mind to ensure in 1970 the growth in the scope of public services in the Far Easter economic region by 2.8 times from 1965, including by 3.3 times in rural areas, and by 3.3 times in Chita region, including by 4.2 times in rural areas.

The Joint Decree of the Central Committee of CPSU and the USSR Council of Ministers No. 561, dated July 8, 1974, and titled "On the Construction of Baikal-Amur Mainline Railway" provided:

- Fixing a regional pay factor of 1.7 on wages of employees during the construction of Baikal-Amur Mainline Railway;
- Extending to employers the benefits fixed for individuals working at localities equivalent to the Far North;
- Paying lump-sum allowances in the amount fixed for regions of the Far North, for dependents of employees transferred, sent or arriving to the construction sites of Baikal-Amur Mainline Railway and BAM-Tynda-Berkakit Railway, including dependents of militaries of the USSR Armed Forces, and dependents of privates and officers of the bodies of USSR Ministry of Interior;
- Payment of wage supplements for mobile work in construction to employees in public service, wholesale, and retail, and catering enterprises, healthcare institutions, kindergartens, public nurseries, housing, and municipal service providers, custodians of residential hotels, employees of clubs, libraries, and propaganda rooms directly engaged in providing services to builders of Baikal-Amur Mainline Railway, second track of Taishet-Lena Railway, and BAM-Tynda-Berkakit Railway;

- Granting of three-year set-up loans (up to 500 rubles per family worker) to employees of construction and installation organizations and enterprises engaged in construction on and servicing of Baikal-Amur Mainline Railway, the second track of Taishet-Lena Railway, and BAM-Tynda-Berkakit Railway;
- Provision of employees with special cold-weather clothes and footwear to provide warmth.

In 1987, the decree "On the Overall Development of Productive Forces in the Far Eastern Economic Region, Buryat ASSR, and Chita Region Until 2000" was signed. As was stated in this document, "acceleration of the overall development of productive forces in the Far Eastern economic region, Buryat ASSR, and Chita region is the specific expression of the Communist party's regional economic policy as developed by the twenty-seventh congress of CPSU, the manifestation of caring to improve the living conditions of workers in this vast territory, and an important part of the party's foreign policy program implementation."

One of the scheduled measures was constructing and commissioning residential houses, preschool institutions, general education schools, hospitals, and out-patient clinics, and the expansion of training general trade workers through constructing and commissioning technical vocational schools.

These documents contributed to an improvement in the image of the Russian Far East and demonstrated the State's interest in using the region's natural wealth and in its healthy social development. The region's population growth during the Soviet period is the evidence of the policy's effectiveness in attracting labor resources to the region and in its development.

However, it should be noted that in the course of settling the Russian Far East the Soviet government also used coercive measures by using the labor of court prisoners; "In 1930s the Soviet government used mass compulsory resettlement and use of labor for court prisoners, including political prisoners. According to 1937's special census, 28% of total registered individuals (i.e., 544 thousand) were in the Far East. Besides convicted persons and persons on trial, this figure included the staff of Cheka administrations, barracked armed security, etc. The greatest percentage of prisoners (57.8% or 314.4 thousand men) was located in the Khabarovsk region, Olkskiy, Severo-Evenskiy, Srednekanskiy territorial districts, and regions of the Far North. The smallest percentage of the prison population was in Kamchatka and Sakhalin."[6]

1.3 RUSSIAN MOTIVATION MODELS INTENDED TO INCREASE THE NUMBER OF ABLE-BODIED POPULATIONS IN THE FAR EASTERN REGION

The transition to market economy mechanisms following the breakdown of the Soviet Union raised the issue of whether spending government funds for the support of remote territories was expedient and whether this region was required within State borders.

The burden of the Far Eastern pay factor and regional pay factor were shifted onto businesses, and prices were unleashed as in the whole country. People started massively emigrating from the region. As a result, from 1989 to 2005 the total population in the Russian Far East reduced by 1,257 thousand (or by 15.8%).

To prevent irreversible effects, the State adopted a number of strategies and programs aimed at the integrated development of this region. However, in the opinion of a number of authors, the documents developed and adopted could not solve (and, indeed, failed to solve) the region's problems.[7]

---

6. *Regional Studies of the Far East: Part 3.* http://pnu.edu.ru/ru/faculties/full_time/uf/iogip/study/studentsbooks/materials/regionovedenie (accessed on 9 June 2020).

7. Savchenko, A. *Why Don't Russian Far East Development Programs Work?* http://www.intelros.ru/pdf/svobodnay_misl/2014_01/8.pdf; Avchenko, V. Strategic impotence. http://expert.ru/2013/10/9/strategicheskoe-bessilie (accessed on 9 June 2020).

In the middle of 1996, the Federal target program "Economic and Social Development of the Russian Far East and Transbaikal Region in 1996–2005" was adopted. In 2002, this program was prolonged until 2010, with another prolongation until 2013 announced in 2007. The only social objective of the program was "to enforce a package of measures aiming to lower social strain in the region." In this case, the objective for this issue was to "develop social infrastructure and retain population in the southern territories of the region." In the opinion of "young reformers," the northern part of the Russian Far East is not economically effective and therefore permanent population is not required there. This, in turn provoked an increase in massive runoff of population from this part of the region. The State saw a resolution of social strain problems in the Russian Far East only in population employment and re-emigration from the Northern territories. Therefore, a package of relevant measures was developed in the program:

- Continuous analysis of the labor market situation;
- Organizing studies of the occupation market's structure and dynamics in the territory of the Russian Far East and Trans-baikal region;
- Developing a system of vocational training and retraining for employed and unemployed individuals in view of the current situation in the local labor market;
- Supporting population groups that are least competitive in the labor market (youth, individuals, parents with many children, pre-retirement persons, handicapped persons, forced migrants, etc.);
- Easing tension in the employment market by supporting the sectors of the regional economic complex that provides the most employment of the population, and the introduction of protectionist measures;

- Developing special programs for the reorganization and liquidation of unprofitable businesses and the development of new employment niches;
- Providing support to small and medium enterprises (SME) and the self-employed in districts, cities, and settlements;
- Developing employment promotion programs (on territorial, region, city, and district levels);
- Setting up regional digital rooms and human resource training centers.

"The package of measures to retain population in the South of the region includes:

- Setting up the system of preferential loans for the population residing in the Southern territories of the Russian Far East and Transbaikal region;
- Improving the population's housing conditions by relocating out of old and failing housing stock;
- Granting loans and credits on preferential conditions to persons who set up workplaces in small business.

The state policy of support for migration from the Northern territories of the Russian Far East shall stipulate the following measures:

- Construction of residential houses for resettlers from the Northern districts of the Russian Far East in new locations (including at the cost and expense of Federal budget);
- Stimulation of migration from districts of the Far North not engaged in economically effective production and expanded use of rotational methods in the colonization of these territories."

Thus, the demographic situation and labor market situation became the region's own problem due to the State setting up its economic priorities without properly taking into account social needs.

By decree of the RF government, No. 801, dated October 21, 2007, some changes were introduced according to which this federal target program was revised for the period until 2013.

Notwithstanding the fact that one of the program objectives was to retain population in the region by preserving and creating new work-places, this issue was not further explored.

In the social sphere framework, the program stipulated a number of measures in education and healthcare only. Thus, in health care it was supposed to:

- Complete construction of a child antituberculosis dispensary in Yakutsk;
- Complete construction of a perinatal center and territorial clinical hospital No. 2 in Khabarovsk;
- Complete construction of a surgical unit at the city clinical hospital and regional children's clinical hospital in Blagovesh-chensk, and a polyclinic in Belogorsk;
- Build a territorial clinical hospital and children's hospital in Petropavlovsk-Kamchatskiy;
- Renovate Central District Hospital at Sobolevo Village (Sobolevo Municipal District) and complete construction of an antitubercu-losis dispensary with an in-patient facility in Palana Settlement;
- Complete construction of a regional clinical hospital's thera-peutic department in the Magadan;
- Complete construction of an oncology dispensary in Yuzhno-Sakhalinsk;
- Build the Children's Restorative Medicine and Rehabilitation Center with an in-patient facility in Birobidzhan and Obluchye District Hospital in Obluchye;
- Complete a package of measures aiming to extend and reno-vate an antituberculosis dispensary in Birobidzhan.

In the education domain, the following measures were proposed:

- Construction of a secondary school in Belgo Village (Komsomolskiy district);
- Complete renovation of a school in Arman Settlement;
- Complete construction of a school in Birobidzhan.

In the culture and sports domain only one measure was planned—the development of Gorny Vozdukh Sports Center.

In 2013, the program was prolonged until 2018 in the federal target program "Economic and Social Development of the Russian Far East and Baikal Region until 2018."

The goal of the program was the development of a transport and power engineering infrastructure in order to ensure the accelerated development of the Russian Far East and Baikal region and improvement of investment climate in the macro-region.

The objectives of the revised program were:

- Development of transport accessibility and improvement of living standards in the territory of the Russian Far East and Baikal region by means of construction and upgrading of regional and local motor roads;
- Provision of timely and secure export of the commodities manufactured in the territory of the Russian Far East, and transported in transit through the territory of the macro-region by a considerable increase in railroad throughput capacity and the development of seaports;
- Setting up a basis for an increase in mobility of the Russian Far East and Baikal region's populations by upgrading regional and local airports.

Thus, the goals of this program did not include a social component, while one of its objectives was to enable the population to leave the region.

The objectives in the framework of labor resource support in the federal target program "Economic and Social Development of the Russian Far East and Baikal Region until 2018" were:

- The development of transport accessibility and improvement of living standards the territory of the Russian Far East and Baikal region by means of construction and upgrading of section of regional and local motor roads;
- Improvement of quality of life in the territory of the Russian Far East and Baikal region by means of development of engineering infrastructure;
- Setting up of a basis for increase in mobility of the population of the Russian Far East and Baikal region by means of upgrading of regional and local airports.

Therefore, the program developers saw that quality of life of the region's population could be improved only by solving the transport problem.

Measures for social sphere development in this program occurred only in the construction of healthcare facilities:

- Construction of a 300-bed surgical facility for the municipal health care institution City Clinical Hospital in Blagoveshchensk;
- Construction of a 250-bed surgical building at Region Governmental Health Care Institution Amur Region Children's Clinical Hospital, in Blagoveshchensk;
- Construction of a 120-bed Obluchye District Hospital plus a polyclinic facility for 240 visits/shift in Obluchye;
- Construction of a paramedical and obstetric station at Ostrovnoye Rural Settlement, Bilibinskiy Municipal District of Chukotka Autonomous area.

Educational, cultural, and sports issues were not considered in the prolonged program version and, therefore, the solution of those issues was not planned.

These programs did not pose questions to solve the demographic situation in the region that was brought up in the strategy. However, in each constituent of the Far Eastern region additional programs were adopted that contributed to the formation of labor resources.

In 2009, by directive of the RF government, the document No. 2094, "Strategy of Social and Economic Development of the Russian Far East and Baikal Region until 2025," dated December 28, 2009, was approved. This document explicitly states the social goals, including those contributing to solution of the demographic problem. Thus, the strategic goal of the Russian Far East development is "to implement the geopolitical aim consisting in retaining the population in the Russian Far East by means of promoting an advanced economy and comfortable living environment in the Russian Federation constituents located in the territory, and achieving an average Russian level of social and economic development."

For the achievement of this goal, the following social objectives were set:

- Formation of a sustainable settlement system based on regional higher-than-market economic growth zones with a comfortable living environment;
- Reduction of barriers hampering economic and social integration of the Far Eastern territory with other regions of Russia;
- Getting population and labor resources in the amount required for addressing economic objectives available in the region, and the improvement of quality of human capital assets;
- Preservation and support of the traditional way of life of indigenous minorities in the Russian Federation.

The Strategy "provides the definition of a package of measures aimed at retaining an able-bodied population in the territory of the Russian Far East and Baikal region and the attraction of a highly-qualified workforce into these regions, including improvement of social infrastructure, development, and improvement of reliability of utility systems in the settlements, improvement of the system of guarantees and compensations for residents in the regions of the Far North, pension provision for the population, and development of vocational education.

In the mid-term and long-term perspectives, key factors of the Russian Far East and Baikal region development will be the preservation and development of labor resources by means of effective internal redistribution of labor resources, attraction, and retention of the workforce from other constituents of the Russian Federation and foreign countries, and improvements in labor force quality."

"The goal of social infrastructure development will be setting up a system of affordable and first-rate higher education, improving access to specialized, including high-technology, health care, support in setting up developed regional and local infrastructure in health care, social security, educational, cultural, and leisure activities, assistance in providing citizens with comfortable housing and communal services, and stimulating the transformation of the living environment.

Moreover, the quality and availability of the services should exceed the national average in order to compensate for unfavorable natural, climatic, and geographical living conditions."

"The federal policy in education in the territory of the Russian Far East and Baikal region will be aimed at ensuring availability of pre-school education, improvement in quality of the general education system, restoration of elementary and secondary vocational education and supplementary education, and the development of higher education. Moreover, a continuing education system will be set up."

"The goal of healthcare system development is to increase life expectancy in the population, reduce infant, child, and maternal mortality, and reduce the morbidity rate."

"The goal of cultural sector development in the Russian Far East and Baikal region is to develop and achieve the potential of the whole society and every individual."

"The national policy in physical culture and sports will be aimed at increasing the interest of the Russian Far East and Baikal region residents in regular exercise and sporting activities, and the popularization of sports as the basis for a healthy lifestyle."

"In furtherance of the State policy regarding social support of the Russian Far East and Baikal region population, state guarantees will be provided to the most vulnerable social groups with a social service market beginning to be set up and a package of measures aimed at laying the material and organizational basis for a social protection system meeting current living standards."

"For the population of the Russian Far East and Baikal region, the cost of air and railroad transport services will be lowered by subsidizing ticket prices."

"The most important direction of the Russian Far East and Baikal region's social and economic development is the assistance in providing the population with comfortable housing and public utility services, and stimulating the transformation of the living environment."

"One of the additional mechanisms ensuring retention of the Russian Far East and Baikal region population will be providing the citizens of the Russian Federation who reside or intend to reside in this territory with benefits in the form of a one-time free allocation of a maximum 0.3 ha land plot for single-family residence construction."

"The main development trends in the housing and utilities sector will consist in improving the quality of public utility services, reduction of cost in service providers and, the resulting reduction of service tariffs while maintaining quality standards for the services provided, and mitigation for the residents of the process of reforming the system of rental housing payment and public utility charges."

"Additional measures will be taken aiming to stimulate the resettlement of Russian expatriates to the constituent entities of the Russian Federation located in the territory of the Russian Far East and Baikal region."

In 2013, the federal target program "Economic and Social Development of the Russian Far East and Baikal Region for the Period until 2025" was developed with the program timeline from 2015 to 2025.

The goal of the program was "the acceleration of the Russian Far East and Baikal region's social and economic development with a focus on the implementation of export potential."

One of the program's objectives was "to develop human potential for the purposes of the program's staffing." Thus, the State is interested in resolving the region's staffing problems only to the extent of the staffing needs outlined in the measures under this program aimed at implementing export potential. Moreover, indicators of human capital development will be the "number of created vacancies" and the "number of new resettlers."

In this program, the development of human capital was suggested to be implemented at a world-class level, with the attraction of international actors with the use of state-of-the-art achievements in the educational and personnel training fields. A number of the following measures were suggested to achieve this goal:

- Training of professional managers for territories of the Russian Far East and Baikal region;
- Training of highly-qualified professional workers;
- Streamlining of the mechanism of personnel selection for governmental and municipal service;
- Supporting the resettlement of Russian Federation citizens and their family members to create the Advanced Social and Economic Development Territories (ASEDT) and implementing investment projects aimed at the social and economic development of these territories;
- Retraining ASEDT's employees;
- Setting up schools in the Asian Pacific region;
- Setting up venture funds and innovative infrastructure.

In addition, specific guarantees are offered to resettlers, namely the compensation of traveling expenses (payment for tickets and transportation of luggage) and the single time subsidy of two months' rent. It must be mentioned that for resettlers in the Tsarist and Soviet Russia a lot more guarantees were provided. This federal program was not approved because the head of the relevant competent ministry changed.

On April 4, 2013, the government approved the State program "Social and Economic Development of the Russian Far East and Baikal Region."[8] The responsible authority in charge of that national program was the RF Ministry for Development of the Russian Far East. The associate authority in charge was the RF Ministry of Regional Development. The timeline of this national program was 2014 to 2025.

The program stipulated the establishment of conditions for accelerated development of the Russian Far East and Baikal region, transformation of the territory into a competitive region with a diversified economy and the improvement of the social and demographical situation in the territory of this macro-region.

This national program included two federal target programs:

- The federal target program titled "Social and Economic Development of the Russian Far East and Baikal Region for the Period until 2018"; and
- The federal target program titled "Social and Economic Development of the Kuril Islands (Sakhalin Region) in 2007–2015";

As well as twelve subprograms, of which five subprograms were aimed at improving the regional population's quality of life:

- "Improvement of Efficiency in the Russian Far East and Baikal Region's Economy"; "Creation of a Comfortable Living Environment for the Population of the Russian Far East and Baikal Region";

---

8. *Executive Order of the RF Government*, (2013). No. 466, Part 1.

- "Environmental Protection and Safety in the Russian Far East and Baikal Region";
- "Scientific and Staffing Support to Implement the Russian Federation National Program 'Social and Economic Development of the Russian Far East and Baikal Region'";
- "Development of Tourism in the Russian Far East and Baikal Region."

The goals of the subprogram titled "Scientific and Staffing Support to Implement the Russian Federation National Program 'Social and Economic Development of the Russian Far East and Baikal Region'" were:

- Ensuring the implementation of the National Program "Social and Economic Development of the Russian Far East and Baikal Region" by qualified personnel;
- Setting up balanced regional vocational education systems that meet the needs of regional employment markets in the macro-region;
- Mitigation of disproportions in the personnel training structure, improvement research activities' efficiency, and the support of federal universities and institutes of the Siberian and Far East branches of the Russian Academy of Sciences;
- Involvement of youth in social practices.

Under the subprogram, the following objectives were set:

- Implementation of measures to determine the needs in building up the material and technological aids and facilities at educational and research institutions depending on the long-term needs of the employment market of the macro-region;
- Implementation of measures to attract specialists from other regions of the Russian Federation and foreign countries into the economy and social sphere of the macro-region;

- Creation and development of major research and educational centers able to ensure breakthroughs in personnel training and the development of innovative technologies for the region's economy;
- Development of distance training;
- Tying-up personnel training processes with demographic waves.

According to this subprogram, since 2014 a four-year sponsorship should be provided on completion for projects developed by vocational education institutions and aimed at upgrading and expanding secondary and higher vocational education programs both in intramural (distant) and intra-mural/extra-mural (evening) forms. Beginning from 2015, the macro-region shall provide support (until 2025 inclusive) of the projects delivered by three to five distance education centers. Plans also included developmental support of public web resources for vocational education programs, including specialized university-based educational portals.

Among all programs adopted in the 1990s and 2000s, our program was the one best aimed at the needs of the population residing in the Far East, and the improvement of living quality.

Development of labor resources was moved to a special subprogram, and scheduled actions had innovative approaches, and took into account current trends in human resource development both in Russia and abroad. This subprogram contained specific and realistic actions mostly based on the region's own resource base, which would contribute to their successful implementation and support by residents of the region.

In April 2014, by decree of the RF Government, No. 308, the RF national program "Social and Economic Development of the Russian Far East and Baikal Region"[9] was approved, which replaced and superseded the former national program. The program's timeline was 2014 to 2025.

---

9. *Executive Order of the RF Government*, (2014). No. 308.

The program's goal was accelerated development of the Russian Far East and Baikal region and improving the social and demographic situation in the Russian Far East and Baikal region. One of the program's objectives was again "improving quality of life in region's territory by means of construction and upgrading sections of regional motor roads" and "setting up the basis for the population's increased mobility." The program includes only one subprogram: "Support for Implementing the RF National Program 'Social and Economic Development of the Russian Far East and Baikal Region' and Other Measures in the Domain of Balanced Territory Development" plus two federal target programs: "Economic and Social Development of the Russian Far East and Baikal Region for the Period until 2018" and "Social and Economic Development of the Kuril Islands (Sakhalin Region) from 2007–2015."

One can mention, as an innovation in the program, the establishment of ANO Human Capital Development Agency (HCDA) in the Russian Far East aiming at organization of provisioning of investors with required personnel. It may be concluded that this program regards the Far Eastern region only as the country's mineral base.

Population problems are addressed secondarily and partially, in terms of necessity, to provide labor resources for relevant projects. This trend may result in irrevocable negative effects with final depopulation of the region, with its residents switching to work on a rotational basis and the absence of a robust permanent population.

In February 2016, a new document titled "The RF National Program 'Social and Economic Development of the Russian Far East and Baikal Region" was developed. This program includes five subprograms and three federal target programs.

One of the program's goals was "to ensure demand in labor resources and retention of the population in the Far East." At that, one of the objectives set is "the attraction of investments and labor resources to the Far East."

One should point out the constituent of the Far Eastern Federal District (FEFD) in which the State's social development approaches manifested themselves the most. The general strategic goal of the Primorskiy territory's administration in years 2001 to 2012 was worded as follows: "To provide in the Primorskiy territory leading national living standards for the economically active population. For that purpose, to create conditions which ensure the preservation and attraction to the territory of highly-efficient development resources, the quality parameters of which will enable increasing regional per capita income by 2.2 times by 2010."[10] "The stage-by-stage implementation of Primorskiy territory's development strategy for years 2001 to 2012 resulted in exponential growth of per capita income in the population, both in Primorskiy territory (by 9.3 times) and in the FEFD as a whole (by 8.2 times)."[11] The APEC Summit held in Vladivostok contributed to the development of both economic and social infrastructure. The newly established Far Eastern Federal University helped to look from a different perspective not only at this region, but at the position of Russia as a whole, which is committed to developing education and science at the global level even in such remote regions. This is also proof of the State's concern as to the healthy development of the FEFD and the enhancement of relations with Asia Pacific countries.

Any further activation of Vladivostok's development is related to the development and implementation of the federal law dated July 13, 2015, No. 212-FZ, titled "On the Free Port of Vladivostok." The last goal set in this legislative act is "the Acceleration of Vladivostok Free Port's Social and Economic Development and Improvement of Living Standards for the Population Residing in the Far Eastern Territory." However, neither mechanisms nor means of

---

10. Darkin, S. M., (2007). *Pacific Russia: Strategy, Economy, Security* (p. 124). Moscow: Delo.
11. Darkin, S. M., (2016). Strategic problems of the Russian Far East. *Management Consulting*, *1*, p. 71.

improving the population's living standards are prescribed further in this document.

Specialized state agencies established in the FEFD will contribute to the boosting of population employment in the region in conditions of its accelerated development.

The first of such agencies was the RF Ministry for Development of the Russian Far East (RF Minvostokrazvitiya),[12] which, as a federal executive authority, coordinates the territory of the FEFD's activities on implementing national programs and federal target programs, manages federal property situated in the territory of the FEFD, and controls the exercise by RF constituents' governmental authorities of the RF state powers granted to those constituents according to the RF laws. The RF Minvostokrazvitiya was established by decree of the RF government, dated June 30, 2012, No. 664.

The Human Capital Development Agency in the Russian Far East (HCDA FE and/or the "Agency") was established as an autonomous non-profit organization according to the directive of the RF government, dated September 2, 2015, No. 1713-p (as amended on December 17, 2015).

The goal of the Agency's activities consists in solving complex issues related to providing the FEFD with labor resources, ensuring positive migratory dynamics by means of additional population inflow, and its retention in the territory.

The Agency's functions are:

- Informational, organizational, and methodological support of measures for attracting workers from other constituents of the Russian Federation;
- Informational, organizational, and methodological support of employees in the field of labor resource provision;

---

12. *Ministry for the Development of the Russian Far East.* http://minvostokrazvitia.ru (accessed on 9 June 2020).

- Full-service support of investment projects as to its labor resource endowment in the territory of the FEFD, and the provision of information on labor market;
- Implementation of projects and initiatives on improving the image of the FEFD as a territory for living in comfort, and for professional and career development;
- Introduction of best practices into the continuing vocational education/training system, and other functions.

ANO HCDA in the Russian Far East developed "The Navigator throws Requested Professions in the Far East 2019–2025."[13] This navigator contains information about existing vacancies to be opened in advanced development territories (ADTs) and at resident enterprises of Vladivostok Free Port during the implementation of investment projects in the Russian Far East.

This navigator shows about 80,000 new vacancies with a planning horizon until 2025, including 25 thousand vacancies that will appear at the resident companies of Accelerated Development Territories, and 18 thousand vacancies that will appear under the Vladivostok Free Port program. This navigator also represents the personnel demand of investment projects initiators in the Russian Far East and a number of existing employers in the macro-region.

To implement the RF Federal Law dated December 29, 2014, No. 473-FZ, titled "On Accelerated Development Territories in the Russian Federation," by decree of the RF government dated April 30, 2015, No. 432, a managing company was established to control and manage ASEDT in the RF constituents within the FEFD pursuant to the order of the RF Ministry for developing the Russian Far East, dated February 27, 2015, No. 20 "On the Approval of the Provision 'On a Supervisory Board of an Advanced Social and Economic Development Territory.'"

---

13. *Navigator of Requested Professions in the Far East 2019–2025.* https://www.hcfe.ru/study-in-the-far-east/navigator/ (accessed on 9 June 2020).

The following issues belong to the competence of a supervisory board:

- Coordination of activities and monitoring fulfillment of the agreement to establish an advanced social and economic development territory;
- Assistance in implementing projects initiated by residents of an advanced social and economic development territory, and projects taken on by other investors in an advanced social and economic development territory;
- Evaluation of an advanced social and economic development territory's operational efficiency;
- Examination and approval of development strategies for an advanced social and economic development territory;
- Monitoring fulfillment of examined and approved plans and strategies;
- Fixing a share of foreign employees engaged by residents in an advanced social and economic development territory.

The Far East and Baikal Region Development Fund was established on the joint initiative of the RF president and the chairman of the RF government. This Fund is a governmental financial development agency and it ensures a flexible approach to project structuring and financing. The Fund makes investments in newly established enterprises and infrastructure facilities that have a significant social and economic effect for the development of the region's economy.

The goals for which the FEFD Development Fund[14] was set up is the search, structuring, and implementation of projects that have a significant multiplicative effect, the creation of new opportunities to attract investments to the Russian Far East, and providing assistance to regional authorities in preparation and structuring of public-private projects (including under concession procedures). One of the Fund's

---

14. *FEFD Development Fund.* http://fondvostok.ru (accessed on 9 June 2020).

objectives is to attract foreign partners with professional competences to the region. The top priority objective for the Fund is cooperation with top companies and financial organizations from the Asia Pacific region, beginning with China, Japan, and the Republic of Korea.

Being a governmental development institution, the Fund acts as a catalyst of investment processes in the region, contributing to accelerated social and economic development of the Far East.

The fund highlights a number of top-priority activities:

- Infrastructure projects in transport and power engineering;
- Support of investment projects that are implemented in the ADTs set up in the Far East;
- Projects in agriculture and bio-resources;
- Projects aimed at developing tourist and recreation areas;
- Projects aimed at industry development in the Far East;
- Projects related to resource development, including mineral extraction and processing.

To increase the FEFD's attractiveness, ADTs are set up; these are territories of the FEFD where, as per the decision of the RF government, special legal regulations are established aimed at creating favorable business and investment conditions.

ADTs are set up for certain businesses that have eased tax burdens, environmental impact audits, and free employment of migrants and preferential health care services. Thus, the local population will have, at best, social losses in the form of growing environmental pollution, taking away land for ADTs, migratory tension, etc. Here an indirect positive social effect is possible in the form of extra commodities manufactured and consumption growth, as well as employment opportunity at workplaces that will be available for Russian citizens. Tax income for the local budget will be minor, since benefits are granted for such businesses.

The plan for filling new jobs in key sectors of the FEFD's economy by graduates of higher education institutions located in the territory of the FEFD (this job substitution plan was developed under "Program of Measures Aimed at Personnel Training for Key Sectors of the FEFD's Economy and Support of Youth in the Employment Market until 2025"[15]) does not represent social services, cultural, science, and educational sectors that can be characterized as a consideration of the region as the mineral base, and not as a territory with decent living standards.

The current policy of attracting labor resources to the Russian Far East is not highly effective. The slowdown of a negative migration balance that is viewed as a positive result of the established government authorities' activities and the implementation of these programs runs parallel to a decline in living standards and real income of the population, a real estate price crash, and a surge in prices for air and railroad tickets that largely prevents populations from leaving the region. Spot projects that are not tied into a system with a holistic and sequential approach will not give a desired positive result in this region's development.

KEYWORDS

> ➤ advanced development territories
> ➤ advanced social and economic development territories
> ➤ Communist Party of the Soviet Union
> ➤ Human Capital Development Agency
> ➤ small and medium enterprises
> ➤ the Russian Far East

---

15. *Executive Order of the RF Government*, (2018). No. 1727.

2 | Trends in Development of the Far Eastern Federal District's Workforce

2.1 LABOR RESOURCE DYNAMICS

In 27 years of market reforms, the region, which makes up 36% of the territory of the Russian state, has lost 23.4% of its residents because of migration, and this tendency remains (Figures 2.1 and 2.2). The population, which left the region within this period, exceeds the number of residents in any million-plus Russian city except Moscow and St. Petersburg. If we consider population density in the Russian Far East and express its surface footage in terms of that population density, one may conclude that in these years Russia lost 1,729,283 m² of its area. This makes about 28% of the FEFD's area or 10% of the territory of Russia.

The greatest part of the region's population resides in Primorskiy territory (Figure 2.2), which is a preferable location due to its natural conditions, climate, and geographical location.

In 2018, the FEFD's administrative center was moved to this constituent, i.e., to Vladivostok. The smallest population is in the Chukotka Autonomous District owing to its very harsh environment, severe climate, and underdeveloped social infrastructure.

The Far Eastern region has sufficient labor potential, with working-age individuals prevailing in its population, although their share gradually decreases in favor of persons below and above working age. Moreover, in 27 years the burden on working-age individuals increased from 56.6% to 71.2% (Figures 2.3–2.5).

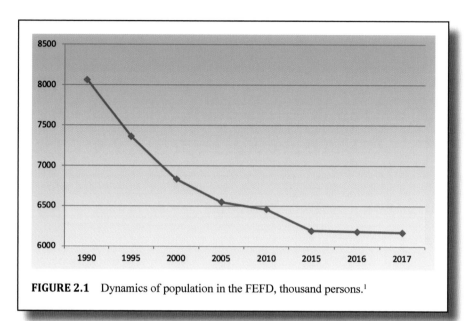

FIGURE 2.1 Dynamics of population in the FEFD, thousand persons.[1]

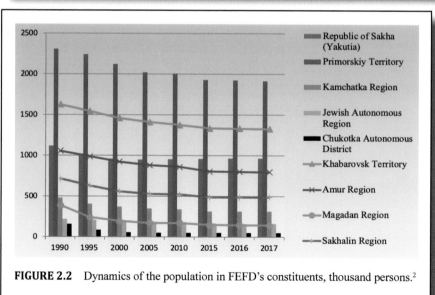

FIGURE 2.2 Dynamics of the population in FEFD's constituents, thousand persons.[2]

1. *Social and Economic Situation of Federal Districts*, (2018). http://www.gks.ru (accessed on 9 June 2020).
2. Regions of Russia, (1992–2018). *Socio-Economic Indicators (1992–2018)*. Statistical compendium, RF Federal Service of State Statistics, Moscow. http://www.gks.ru (accessed on 9 June 2020).

Before 2010, a decrease in the share of individuals below working age was reported (Figure 2.3), but afterwards this figure grew gradually against a continuing decrease in the share of working-age individuals. The maximum share of individuals under working age is observed in the Republic of Sakha (Yakutia), with the minimum reported in Primorskiy territory. Dynamics of this indicator may be treated as a positive trend, since with correct educational policy in the region competitive labor resources can appear.

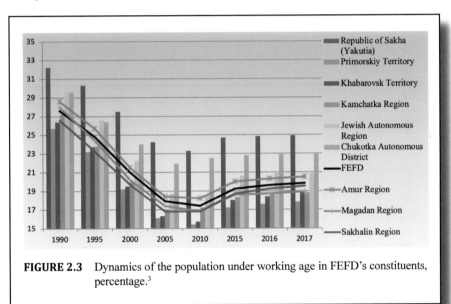

FIGURE 2.3 Dynamics of the population under working age in FEFD's constituents, percentage.[3]

The negative dynamics of the working-age population reflect in the negative trend in FEFD's development (Figure 2.4). The implementation of national projects in the FEFD requires professional personnel, which is against the existing trends, and this situation should be changed radically.

3.   Regions of Russia, (1992–2018). *Socio-Economic Indicators (1992–2017)*. Statistical compendium, RF Federal Service of State Statistics, Moscow, http://www.gks.ru (accessed on 9 June 2020).

A significant and growing share of over-working-age individuals is a burden on the employed population and social infrastructure facilities (Figure 2.5). This situation is somewhat offset by the fact that persons in this age group cannot live on the subsidies provided by the State. Therefore, they have to work and cover the labor deficit in the region. However, the number of these employees is not enough to fill all vacancies, while modern technologies require new skills and abilities that elderly persons can hardly master. Moreover, in some economic sectors, these workers become an obstacle for the promotion of younger employees.

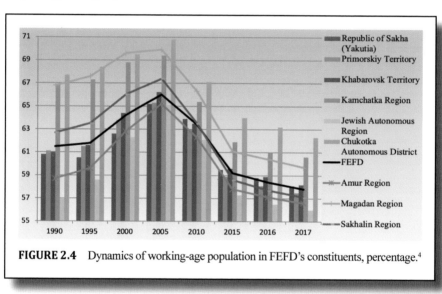

FIGURE 2.4 Dynamics of working-age population in FEFD's constituents, percentage.[4]

The share of above-working-age persons shows a persistent growth trend, with the highest value reported in Primorskiy territory, and the lowest one in the Chukotka Autonomous District.

Changes in the population's age pattern increase the burden on the working-age group, which at the same time faces employment problems in the economy (Table 2.1).

---

4. *Ibid.*

The labor force in the Far Eastern Federal District (FEFD) shrunk by 21% in 27 years. The labor force number fell in all constituents of the region, in particular in the Magadan region, i.e., by 3.6 times. This situation demonstrates sufficiently complicated baseline conditions as to the creation of the region's economic potential.

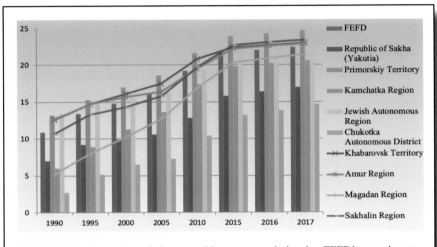

FIGURE 2.5 Dynamics of above working-age population in FEFD's constituents, percentage.[5]

TABLE 2.1 Labor Force Dynamics in FEFD's Constituents, Thousand Persons[6]

	1990	1995	2000	2005	2010	2015	2016	2017
Far Eastern Federal District	4272	3811	3696	3454	3437	3376	3355	3340
Republic of Sakha (Yakutia)	618	575	528	486	494	501	490	498
Kamchatka Territory	248	211	222	207	190	189	183	179
Primorskiy Territory	1147	1092	1084	1067	1071	1057	1049	1036
Khabarovsk Territory	962	767	784.7	748	743	728	734	733
Amur Region	538	544	506	416	429	412	414	414
Magadan Region	326	150	127	101	102	93	90	91
Sakhalin Region	424	436	322	306	288	280	278	276
Jewish Autonomous Region	...	95	86	90	87	85	85	82
Chukotka Autonomous District	...	46	38	33	33	32	32	31

---

5. *Ibid.*
6. *Ibid.*

2.2 EDUCATIONAL POTENTIAL OF LABOR RESOURCES

The educational potential of the FEFD's labor resources is high enough, and it is mainly the heritage of the Soviet era, which tried to develop the region by increasing the education level of its residents. During this time, both classic and specialized educational institutions of various training levels were established.

From the top universities at the country's center, the best professionals were transferred to head Far Eastern institutes and universities, set up departments, and to actively develop science and professional education and training in the Far East.

However, the end of the Soviet era and profound reforms, including in the education system, resulted in a catastrophic situation in the field. The number of educational institutions and major disciplines dropped off (Tables 2.2 and 2.3).

TABLE 2.2 Number of Professional Educational Institutions That Provide Training of Skilled Workers and Office Employees[7] (By End of Year)

	1990	1995	2000	2005	2010	2015
Far Eastern Federal District	219	236	227	207	155	61
Republic of Sakha (Yakutia)	33	32	31	36	29	13
Kamchatka Territory	12	16	15	15	12	1
Primorskiy Territory	64	65	59	43	38	15
Khabarovsk Territory	52	48	49	48	22	11
Amur Region	30	31	29	29	22	6
Magadan Region	8	10	10	10	10	8
Sakhalin Region	20	22	21	15	12	3
Jewish Autonomous Region	8	9	8	7	4	
Chukotka Autonomous District	4	4	3	3	–	

The dynamics of the number of students at state and municipal professional educational institutions studying under mid-level professional

---

7. (Since 2018 this information has not been presented in statistical compendiums.) Regions of Russia, (1992–2018). *Socio-Economic Indicators: 1992–2018.* Statistical compendium, RF Federal Service of State Statistics, Moscow. http://www.gks.ru (accessed on 9 June 2020).

training programs per 10,000 residents of the FEFD exceeds all-Russia figures (Figure 2.6). In 2015, the FEFD was at the top position in the Russian Federation by this indicator. That is, in the region a big stratum of people formed with occupations that meet the needs of the labor market in the region (Tables 2.3 and 2.4).

TABLE 2.3 Number of Professional Educational Institutions That Provide Training of Mid-Level Professionals[8] (By End of Academic Year)

	1990/ 1991	1995/ 1996	2000/ 2001	2005/ 2006	2010/ 2011	2015/ 2016	2016/ 2017	2017/ 2018
Far Eastern Federal District	133	137	137	132	125	153	196	199
Republic of Sakha (Yakutia)	18	20	22	28	31	40	49	49
Kamchatka Territory	6	7	7	8	8	9	12	13
Primorskiy Territory	34	35	32	27	25	40	48	49
Khabarovsk Territory	29	28	28	26	28	28	37	35
Amur Region	23	23	23	23	14	10	13	14
Magadan Region	5	6	4	4	4	5	11	11
Sakhalin Region	11	10	12	10	9	12	15	15
Jewish Autonomous Region	6	6	6	5	5	5	8	9
Chukotka Autonomous District	1	1	3	1	1	4	3	4

TABLE 2.4 Number of Higher Education Institutions and Research Institutions[9] (By End of Academic Year)

	1990/ 1991	1995/ 1996	2000/ 2001	2005/ 2006	2010/ 2011	2015/ 2016	2016/ 2017	2017/ 2018
Far Eastern Federal District	32	46	51	49	51	38`	35	35
Republic of Sakha (Yakutia)	2	4	5	8	9	7	7	7
Kamchatka Territory	10	14	4	3	3	2	2	2
Primorskiy Territory	11	12	13	12	13	9	8	8
Khabarovsk Territory	4	4	18	17	17	12	10	10
Amur Region	2	4	4	5	5	4	4	4
Amur Region	2	4	4	5	5	4	4	4
Magadan Region	1	1	1	1	1	1	1	1
Sakhalin Region	1	6	5	2	2	2	2	2
Jewish Autonomous Region	1	1	1	1	1	1	1	1

---

8. *Ibid.* (Since 2016, including organizations engaged in training of skilled works and office employees.)
9. *Ibid.*

The number of students studying under bachelor degree, master degree, and specialist programs per 10,000 residents in the FEFD are less than in Russia at average (Figure 2.7). The number of students started to grow again after a long decrease, particularly in Primorskiy and Khabarovsk territories. In 2017, the above indicator continued to decrease in the Amur region, the Jewish Autonomous region, and the Kamchatka territory.

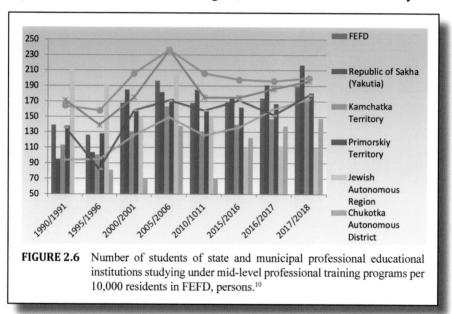

FIGURE 2.6 Number of students of state and municipal professional educational institutions studying under mid-level professional training programs per 10,000 residents in FEFD, persons.[10]

2.3 QUALITATIVE CHARACTERISTICS OF POPULATION EMPLOYMENT

The dynamics of population employment in the FEFD is presented on Figure 2.8.[11] After an abrupt decrease in the number of employed in the

10. Compiled by the author on the basis of data from the statistical compendium "Regions of Russia, (2018). *Socio-Economic Indicators*. http://www.gks.ru/bgd/regl/b15_14p/Main. htm (accessed on 9 June 2020). (Since 2016, including institutions that provide training of skilled workers and office employees.)

11. Here and in Tables 2.5–2.7, data for years 2015 to 2016 are calculated according to an updated procedure of calculating the labor resource balance and labor cost estimation. The increase in the average annual number of employed individuals in the majority of RF constituents is due to changes in the estimate of payroll employees employed by organizations and individual entrepreneurs not covered within the statistical survey.

economy in the 90s, the situation practically stabilized and now keeps within certain numerical ranges. The largest number of employed persons, which corresponds to the share of working-age persons, is observed in Primorskiy territory, while the least number is seen in the Chukotka Autonomous region.

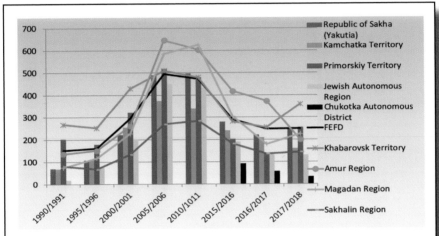

FIGURE 2.7   Number of students studying under bachelor, specialist, or master degree programs per 10,000 residents as of beginning of academic year in FEFD.[12]

In the FEFD, a great number of various enterprises with various ownership forms operate in various activities. The distribution of employees by enterprises is as follows (Tables 2.5 and 2.6).

The number of the employed in 2017 increased only in mining enterprises (the growth in the number of employed resumed after a decade-long fall due to the region's implementation of the Law on advanced development territories (ADTs) that primarily deals with mining businesses), processing, construction industries, hotels, and restaurants. In other sectors, the employment reduction trend in 2017 remained.

---

12. Compiled by the author on the basis of data of the statistical compendium "Regions of Russia, (2018). *Socio-Economic Indicators*." http://www.gks.ru/bgd/regl/b15_14p/Main.htm (accessed on 9 June 2020).

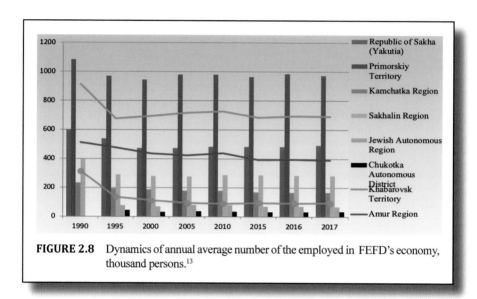

FIGURE 2.8 Dynamics of annual average number of the employed in FEFD's economy, thousand persons.[13]

TABLE 2.5 Dynamics of Distribution of the Employed in FEFD, by Economic Activity, Thousand Persons[14]

Economic Activity	2000	2005	2010	2015	2016	2017
Agriculture, hunting, and forestry	363.8	318.7	307.3	230.2	235.4	224.6
Mining	110.3	115.9	109.9	109.6	113.6	115.2
Processing sector	347.2	317.9	283.3	268.1	268.5	271.0
Production and distribution of electric energy, gas, and water	137.4	158.1	153.3	147.4	147.3	129.8
Construction	186.8	217.0	260	282.8	281.4	286.0
Wholesale and retail trade; repairs of cars, motorcycles, household goods and personal articles	480.1	555.1	557.7	537.3	562.3	553.0
Hotels and restaurants	44.4	61.9	60.5	70.5	70.6	72
Transport and telecom	353.1	356.8	336.6	335.6	341.0	295.6
Education	332.1	329.9	306.3	281.0	280.7	279.2
Health care and social services	233.1	235.1	232.3	225.4	224.9	215.6
Real estate transactions	212.8	210	242.7	250.1	245.3	73.6
Provision of other public utility, social, and personal services	107.7	117.8	122.4	122.0	119.5	–
Other activities	253.7	268.3	328.9	320.4	312.9	584.1

13. Regions of Russia, (1992–2018). *Socio-Economic Indicators: 1992–2018*. Statistical compendium, RF Federal Service of State Statistics, Moscow. http://www.gks.ru (accessed on 9 June 2020).
14. Calculated by the author on the basis of data from the statistical compendium "Regions of Russia. *Socio-Economic Indicators 2011–2018*." http://www.gks.ru/bgd/regl/b15_14p/Main.htm (accessed on 9 June 2020).

TABLE 2.6 Structure of the Overall Workforce in the FEFD's Economy Across Age Groups, Percentage[15]

Year	Total	Including in the Age, Years						Average Age, Years
		Under 20*	20 to 29	30 to 39	40 to 49	50 to 59	60 and More	
2005								
FEFD	100	2.2	23.6	24.5	27.7	18.4	3.6	39.8
Republic of Sakha (Yakutia)	100	2.9	22.3	25.7	30.4	15.3	3.5	40.0
Kamchatka Territory	100	2.2	24.2	24.9	26.9	18.2	3.7	39.8
Primorskiy Territory	100	1.7	24.6	24.2	26.5	19.2	3.8	40.0
Khabarovsk Territory	100	2.9	21.5	24.9	29.2	18.9	2.7	40.8
Amur Region	100	1.9	24.1	25.8	27.4	17.9	2.9	39.8
Magadan Region	100	1.6	21.9	24.0	29.1	20.4	3.1	39.3
Sakhalin Region	100	2.4	24.0	20.8	27.9	20.1	4.9	40.3
Jewish Autonomous Region	100	1.2	22.6	24.1	26.5	21.3	4.3	40.3
Chukotka Autonomous District	100	1.8	22.4	24.4	30.7	18.2	2.5	37.3
2010								
FEFD	100	1.2	23.4	25.7	24.5	20.3	4.9	39.9
Republic of Sakha (Yakutia)	100	1.4	22.9	25.5	27.6	19.3	3.4	39.6
Kamchatka Territory	100	0.9	22.7	26.5	24.4	19.3	6.1	40.2
Primorskiy Territory	100	1.1	22.7	25.7	24.0	20.4	6.0	40.3
Khabarovsk Territory	100	1.1	24.9	25.4	23.4	19.8	5.3	39.7
Amur Region	100	1.6	25.5	26.1	23.8	19.7	3.2	38.9
Magadan Region	100	0.7	20.7	24.6	25.0	24.1	4.9	41.0
Sakhalin Region	100	1.3	21.6	25.3	24.6	22.5	4.7	40.4
Jewish Autonomous Region	100	0.9	23.7	27.1	23.9	20.7	3.6	39.6
Chukotka Autonomous District	100	1.6	20.8	24.4	25.9	22.9	4.4	40.7
2017								
FEFD	100	0.5	20.7	28.0	24.0	19.8	7.0	40.8
Republic of Sakha (Yakutia)	100	0.4	22.1	27.5	23.4	20.7	5.8	40.4
Kamchatka Territory	100	0.5	19.5	29.4	25.2	18.4	6.9	40.7
Primorskiy Territory	100	0.3	20.0	27.6	24.6	20.4	7.1	41.1
Khabarovsk Territory	100	0.5	22.1	28.2	23.4	18.5	7.2	40.5
Amur Region	100	0.9	21.9	28.3	23.5	19.2	6.1	40.2
Magadan Region	100	0.4	16.6	27.7	23.5	22.0	9.9	42.5
Sakhalin Region	100	0.4	17.7	28.3	24.7	20.0	8.8	41.8
Jewish Autonomous Region	100	0.4	18.9	28.5	24.5	20.9	6.8	41.2
Chukotka Autonomous District	100	0.6	17.0	28.4	25.4	22.8	5.8	41.4

15. Compiled by the author on the basis of data of the statistical compendium "Regions of Russia. *Socio-Economic Indicators 2011–2018*." http://www.gks.ru/bgd/regl/b15_14p/Main.htm (accessed on 9 June 2020). (In 2015 and 2016 this group includes individuals aged under 19.)

A significant share of the FEFD's economy is taken by wholesale and retail trade and repairs of cars, motorcycles, household goods, and personal articles. In seventeen years, the share of employed in this sector increased from 17 to 19%.

The second position belongs to employed persons in transport and communication sectors, although their share fell by 1% point. The share of individuals employed in education and manufacturing sectors fell by 3% points.

In 2017, in the FEFD's labor market, persons aged 30 to 39 years prevailed (28.0%), while in 2005 the largest share of the employed belonged to the 40 to 49 year age group (27.7%). There is a steady trend towards reduction of youth among the employed, with an increase of the share of persons aged above 60. In the observed period, the average age of the employed rose from 39.8 years to 40.8 years. The largest average age of the employed is observed in the Magadan region (42.5 years). The highest share of youth in 2017 among the employed was in the Khabarovsk territory and the Republic of Sakha (Yakutia) at 22.1%.

The distribution of the employed by education level is as follows (Table 2.7).

In the FEFD, the all-Russian trend in the employment structure by education level is observed. The share of persons with higher education has grown from 23.6 to 33.5%. The share of persons with compulsory education, or only or no education at all, fell by more than half in the observed period. This trend also corresponds to the age structure of the employed and personnel training dynamics in the region. The highest share of the employed with higher education is reported in Kamchatka territory (40.6% in 2017, which is an increase of 16% in the reviewed period), while the lowest share is in the Jewish Autonomous region (24.9% in 2017). Jewish Autonomous region is in the last position in the FEFD according to living standards and quality of life. In view of future improvements in personnel training policy, it is expected that this trend will change toward an increase in the share of persons holding secondary education.

TABLE 2.7 Dynamics of Structure of the Employed in FEFD's Economy by Education Level, Percentage[16]

Year	Total	Including Having Education				
		Higher	**Secondary**	**General Secondary**	**Basic**	**No Basic**
2005						
Far Eastern Federal District	100	23.6	26.5	22.3	6.2	0.5
Republic of Sakha (Yakutia)	100	25.0	26.2	26.2	4.9	0.6
Kamchatka Territory	100	24.1	21.9	19.9	6.0	0.5
Primorskiy Territory	100	30.2	34.3	15.7	6.4	0.5
Khabarovsk Territory	100	15.4	24.8	35.2	6.1	0.2
Amur Region	100	20.4	24.6	21.4	7.4	0.3
Magadan Region	100	23.2	29.8	26.0	4.0	0.0
Sakhalin Region	100	18.3	26.5	22.7	4.9	0.6
Jewish Autonomous Region	100	18.9	23.6	25.9	16.7	0.7
Chukotka Autonomous District	100	21.0	23.4	20.0	7.4	1.3
2010						
Far Eastern Federal District	100	27.7	26.4	18.8	5.1	0.4
Republic of Sakha (Yakutia)	100	26.8	26.5	23.7	3.6	0.3
Kamchatka Territory	100	32.1	25.8	16.7	3.5	0.2
Primorskiy Territory	100	28.9	25.8	14.8	5.2	0.3
Khabarovsk Territory	100	31.7	25.2	18.3	4.7	0.4
Amur Region	100	22.8	30.1	20.0	7.4	0.6
Magadan Region	100	30.3	20.7	34.0	2.5	0.1
Sakhalin Region	100	21.0	28.5	18.3	4.4	0.4
Jewish Autonomous Region	100	15.7	24.8	26.1	11.6	0.7
Chukotka Autonomous District	100	25.4	25.5	21.5	5.1	0.4
2017						
Far Eastern Federal District	100	33.5	24.1	19.0	4.1	0.4
Republic of Sakha (Yakutia)	100	33.4	24.1	23.0	3.4	0.3
Kamchatka Territory	100	40.6	23.0	17.3	2.8	0.3
Primorskiy Territory	100	33.6	24.1	17.2	4.0	0.3
Khabarovsk Territory	100	35.1	23.8	18.5	4.2	0.2
Amur Region	100	30.9	24.7	16.8	5.4	0.6
Magadan Region	100	33.5	23.8	27.2	2.3	0.1
Sakhalin Region	100	30.9	26.1	20.4	3.9	0.9
Jewish Autonomous Region	100	24.9	22.1	21.8	9.9	1.1
Chukotka Autonomous District	100	34.6	22.2	20.8	4.2	0.4

16. Compiled by the author on the basis of data from the statistical compendium "Regions of Russia. *Socio-Economic Indicators 2011–2018*." http://www.gks.ru/bgd/regl/b15_14p/Main.htm (accessed on 9 June 2020).

Unfortunately, the official statistical database does not contain information about the number of employed individuals holding doctoral and doctoral candidate degrees who form the basis for scientific and technical development in the region.

The dynamics of the employment structure in the economy by ownership status is presented in Table 2.8. The analysis of employment distribution among enterprises of various property statuses can help to distinguish the following trends:

TABLE 2.8 Dynamics of Employment Structure in FEFD's Economy by Ownership Form, Percentage[17]

Year	Total	Including by Ownership Form					
		State-Owned	Munic-ipal	Private	Ownership of Public and Religious Organizations	Mixed	Foreign, Joint Russian and Foreign
2005							
Far Eastern Federal District	100	34.3	23.0	28.7	0.3	11.1	2.6
Republic of Sakha (Yakutia)	100	35.9	28.4	17.5	0.3	17.4	0.4
Kamchatka Territory	100	36.6	26.4	27.3	0.1	9.1	0.4
Primorskiy Territory	100	32.2	19.7	35.1	0.4	9.9	2.7
Khabarovsk Territory	100	34.4	21.2	27.6	0.2	13.3	3.2
Amur Region	100	37.6	25.3	30.4	0.4	3.6	2.7
Magadan Region	100	30.9	25.6	29.0	0.3	11.8	2.3
Sakhalin Region	100	27.4	22.6	34.1	0.4	9.8	5.7
Jewish Autonomous Region	100	44.6	24.5	19.6	0.4	7.2	3.7
Chukotka Autonomous District	100	50.6	22.3	15.4	0.1	8.8	2.9
2010							
Far Eastern Federal District	100	34.4	20.0	34.7	0.3	6.7	3.9
Republic of Sakha (Yakutia)	100	30.7	28.0	25.6	0.3	13.4	2.0

17. Compiled by the author on the basis of data from the statistical compendium "Regions of Russia. *Socio-Economic Indicators 2011–2018*." http://www.gks.ru/bgd/regl/b15_14p/Main.htm (accessed on 9 June 2020).

TABLE 2.8   *(Continued)*

Year	Total	Including by Ownership Form					
		State-Owned	Munic-ipal	Private	Ownership of Public and Religious Organizations	Mixed	Foreign, Joint Russian and Foreign
Kamchatka Territory	100	37.6	22.7	36.0	0.1	2.4	1.2
Primorskiy Territory	100	35.0	16.9	38.4	0.3	5.1	4.3
Khabarovsk Territory	100	35.5	16.8	36.0	0.2	7.9	3.6
Amur Region	100	36.0	20.5	34.8	0.3	3.4	5.0
Magadan Region	100	34.4	22.9	32.6	0.2	7.9	2.1
Sakhalin Region	100	27.4	19.7	41.2	0.3	4.7	6.7
Jewish Autonomous Region	100	42.8	21.3	26.5	0.4	3.7	5.4
Chukotka Autonomous District	100	49.0	22.3	18.2	0.6	4.2	5.7
2017							
Far Eastern Federal District	100	33.4	14.5	41.8	0.2	5.4	4.6
Republic of Sakha (Yakutia)	100	31.5	21.3	31.7	0.2	12.7	2.7
Kamchatka Territory	100	39.1	15.9	41.1	0.1	2.6	1.2
Primorskiy Territory	100	35.1	11.2	45.1	0.2	3.5	4.9
Khabarovsk Territory	100	30.2	11.8	48.4	0.1	5.6	3.8
Amur Region	100	34.8	12.5	43.8	0.3	3.1	5.4
Magadan Region	100	35.2	15.9	37.4	0.1	6.6	4.8
Sakhalin Region	100	31.2	18.0	38.1	0.2	3.3	9.2
Jewish Autonomous Region	100	46.5	18.8	25.0	0.4	2.5	6.8
Chukotka Autonomous District	100	35.8	22.9	25.6	–	2.4	10.9

In the last 13 years, the share of employees at state-owned enterprises grew, while the share of employees at municipal enterprises reduced. The share of private enterprises prevailing in the economy structure grows slowly. Besides, the share of employees at private enterprises in the FEFD is lower than the national average. A similar situation occurs with the share of employees at foreign and joint Russian-foreign enterprises.

In conditions of labor resource shortages, employers express their demand via claimed needs for employees submitted to government-owned employment agencies (Figure 2.9).

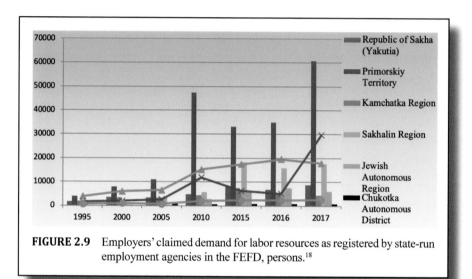

FIGURE 2.9 Employers' claimed demand for labor resources as registered by state-run employment agencies in the FEFD, persons.[18]

As seen in the diagram of the FEFD's labor market, after the launch of the projects related to ADTs the demand for labor resources significantly grew in these constituents of the region, particularly in the Amur region and Primorskiy territory.

Supply in the FEFD's labor market is formed from the Russian citizens residing in the region and migrants from neighboring countries and beyond. In 2017, 24,583 foreign citizens had work permits, which is 3.2 times less than the respective figure in 2011. This decrease is due to a weakened ruble exchange rate, changes in migration and labor laws, and conditions of labor migrants' engagement.

---

18. Compiled by the author on the basis of data from the statistical compendium "Regions of Russia. *Socio-Economic Indicators 2011–2018*." http://www.gks.ru/bgd/regl/b15_14p/Main.htm (accessed on 9 June 2020).

Among the claimed worker jobs, employers' demand is high for specialists in the field of construction, agriculture, forest-industry complex, and trade (bricklayer, carpenter, plasterer, concrete worker, painter, facing worker, floor tiler, logger, driver, tractor operator, salesman, and cook). The main reasons why the above vacancies are not filled are: heavy conditions of work performed; low wages; and working beyond place of residence (at timber logging sites). The demand for skilled workers and office employees is seen for such professions as a sales agent, bookkeeper, and physician.

2.4 POPULATION MIGRATION

Labor resources of the Far Eastern region originally formed under the active influence of migration processes, including international ones. Targeted colonization of these territories in the Tsarist era was parallel to the growth of expatriate employees' engagement. Chinese and Korean workers worked in many industries and economy sectors. In the Soviet period, the development of the Russian Far East was accompanied by national programs aimed at attracting labor resources to the region from other parts of the country (Young Communist construction projects, Baikal Amur Mainline, use of preferential tax treatment, installation grants, additional material support of residents, etc.). The events of 1990s accompanied with the crisis in the state economy and politics resulted in the collapse of many strategic projects in which labor resources had been engaged. The breakdown of the Soviet Union was the catalyst to setting up flows of reverse migrants who were natives of former Soviet Republics, such as the Ukraine, Belarus, etc.

The economic crisis of 2008 aggravated the situation with population migration in the FEFD. During this time, the region fell into migration loss range (Figure 2.10).

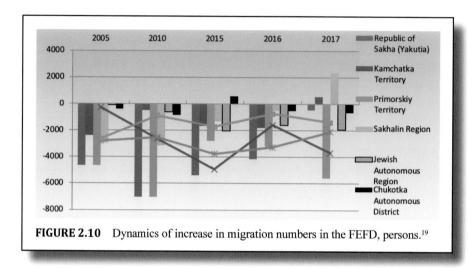

FIGURE 2.10   Dynamics of increase in migration numbers in the FEFD, persons.[19]

In the studied period, the largest negative migration growth was observed in the Republic of Sakha (Yakutia) and Primorskiy territory, each making up 28% of total migration loss in the FEFD. This situation was due to the State's decision to erect potential hazardous production facilities in the region, and the decline in living standards. The workforce is engaged in construction on a rotational basis, therefore active inflow of migrants is accompanied with similar active outflow from the region. The lowest negative migration growth was seen in the Chukotka Autonomous District. In the studied period, migration growth was positive only in Primorskiy territory in 2010–2011, when this Russian Federation constituent was preparing for the Far Eastern APEC Summit.

Migration inflow to the Russian Far East can be broken down into three sources: migrants from other regions of Russia; fellow nationals residing abroad; and foreign immigrants. The second group of migrants differs from the others in that they have the most favorable attraction

---

19. Compiled by the author on the basis of data from the statistical compendium *"Population Size and Migration in the Russian Federation in 2009–2018."* http://www.gks.ru (accessed on 9 June 2020).

conditions. The State guarantees to fellow countrymen a wide set of benefits and preferences. It is assumed that this group of migrants arrives into this region for permanent residence. Therefore, for every potential immigrant first it is checked if he or she can get employment later.

A. V. Ostrovskiy states, "In the estimation of Russian demographic analysts, the FEFD makes up about 10% of all foreign workers present in Russia, with most working migrants from China, KPDR, and Vietnam. These foreign workers are mainly in Primorskiy territory, Khabarovsk territory, and Amur region where they are engaged in construction, agriculture, and the timber industry."[20]

In eight years of the studied period until 2010, all of the region's constituents showed negative migration growth, which afterwards changed to positive migration growth. In 2014, the indicators started to decrease again, with a growth trend seen only in Primorskiy territory, the Republic of Sakha (Yakutia), and Sakhalin region. This was due to the State actively participating in the development of the FEFD's territories, the development of special programs, enactments, etc. The most attractive for migrants was Primorskiy territory (29.5% of all migrants arriving into the region in 2017) and Khabarovsk territory (21.6%).

The least attractive were Chukotka Autonomous district (1.7%) and Jewish Autonomous region (1.7%) in 2017. The leaders in attraction of intra-Russian migrants are Khabarovsk territory (23.4%) and Primorskiy territory (22.5%) in 2017. The number of migrants to these regions exceeds by several times the number of migrants to the least attractive regions of the Far East. Dynamics of these indicators in 2017 compared to 2016 was negative in all of the region's constituents, except Amur region and the Magadan region as well as the Chukotka Autonomous district.

---

20 Ostrovskiy, A. V., (2010). *The Far Eastern Region and Socio-Economic Space: Modernization of Russia as the Prerequisite Condition of its Successful Development in the 21st Century* (p. 308). Moscow: Russian Political Encyclopedia (ROSSPEN).

Trend changes in Primorskiy and Khabarovsk territories in 2014–2015 were mainly due to a sharp decrease in migrants arriving from other regions. The steep decline in 2010 was due to a widening of the economic crisis. The second decline in 2013–2014 was the result of the suspension of various projects because of exchange rate changes. Further growth of migration figures continued until 2014, when migration again started to fall except for figures characterizing migration to the Republic of Sakha (Yakutia).

The highest inflow of migrants is from the Siberian Federal district, mainly because the latter borders with the FEFD. A significant flow of migrants from Central Federal District is due to the opening of central company branch offices in the region, and the transfer of local companies under the umbrella of the Moscow ones.

The age structure of migrants arriving into the FEFD shows the prevalence of working-age individuals, i.e., over 70%. The highest share of working-age individuals was observed in the migrants coming to Kamchatka territory and Chukotka Autonomous district. Severe climate and the remoteness of job sites from main social infrastructure facilities reduce opportunities for the migration of individuals under and over working age to these constituents. The general growth trend of the share of the working-age population began to reverse in 2012. People started to arrive to the region in families, with a high proportion of unemployable-age persons. The growth trend of this figure in 2017 was observed in the Jewish Autonomous region only.

Among persons coming to the FEFD from other regions of Russia, working-age persons prevail, too. In the last ten years, the share of such individuals has ranged between 70 and 80%. The highest share of arriving working-age persons in 2017 was seen in the Jewish Autonomous region.

The structure of immigrants and their education varies based on their arrival territory. The lowest share of individuals with higher education was seen in the Jewish Autonomous region and this number has been gradually reducing. The average share of such individuals in the FEFD was 25.9% in 2017. Their highest share in 2017 was observed in the Chukotka Autonomous District (36.6%), which is the leader among the FEFD's constituents by share of attracted individuals with such education level. The second best is the Magadan region (30.6% in 2017). This is due to the high demand in these regions for highly skilled single-subject specialists who cannot be trained in the territory. In 2017, 86 people with Doctor of Science degrees and 190 doctoral candidates in sciences were brought to the FEFD in total. The top constituents of the FEFD's provinces by this figure were Primorskiy territory, Khabarovsk territory, and Amur region. No doctor of science came to Magadan region. This situation is even worse because invited specialists are shown in the statistical reports of educational and research organizations, but are not always full-time employees that are actually engaged in teaching or research work throughout the academic year in the region. They are mainly employed under short-term contracts that are renewed annually, and thus these employees are shown in statistics as invited migrants with an academic degree. This is also confirmed with migration growth figures; thus, in 2017 migration growth was positive only in three constituents: Amur region, Sakhalin region, and Chukotka Autonomous district (however, this gain amounted only to two or three specialists with a doctoral candidate or doctoral degree). The highest negative migration growth was seen in 2017 in the Khabarovsk region, amounting to sixteen doctoral candidates and five doctors of science. Another problem is the so-called "phantom" employees, i.e., professors who agreed to only be registered in an organization's personnel records in order to meet accreditation requirements. Such "phantom" employees do not take part in the academic process, and are not known to students, graduates, or the majority of lecturers. Of course, all requirements of the law to ensure education quality in the region are met, but in reality, this shatters the population's confidence in education in the Far Eastern

Region, and creates fraudulent schemes. However, it is necessary to note that salary requirements make the employment of highly-paid professors in organizations located in Russian Far East unprofitable. For accreditation, it is enough to employ a doctor of science at a quarter time, therefore it does not pay to employ a doctor of science on a full-time basis and pay a salary to him or her. Moreover, in this case, the quality of the educational process and research activities are out of the question. This is one of the stumbling blocks for the development of the Far East.

The share of migrants holding secondary vocational education in the FEFD ranges between 15 and 36%. The lead regions for attracting such migrants in 2008 were Kamchatka territory and the Jewish Autonomous region. However, in 2017 they were next-to-last and last among the constituents of FEFD. Thus, in 2009 the share of migrants to the Jewish Autonomous region who had this education level was 35.8% as compared to only 17.2% in 2015. This was due to changes in the direction of development of the FEFD's constituents. The share of individuals with a general (complete) secondary education in 2017 was 24% as the FEFD's average indicator, with the highest figure (34.8%) seen in the Republic of Sakha (Yakutia), and the lowest one (11.1%) in Kamchatka territory.

The dynamics of foreign migration has more irregular trends that actively show changes in the economic, financial, and political situation both in the FEFD and in Russia as a whole.

The growth of the State's interest in developing the region was stimulated by an increase of foreign investments into the region and, respectively, a growth in the number of foreign migrants coming to the region. Khabarovsk territory accounted for 30.8% of foreign visitors in 2017, compared to 27.1% in Primorskiy territory, and 42.1% in other constituents of the FEFD. The dynamics of migrant flow to the FEFD's constituents from commonwealth of independent states (CIS) show the priority of Kamchatka territory (37.7%) and Sakhalin region (47.6%) in 2017.

The total growth of foreign migrants to constituents of the FEFD, except CIS states, is negative (-440 persons). The highest figure is shown in Primorskiy territory (-1302 persons), which is due to the termination of high-scope government projects in this constituent and reduced demand in the additional foreign workforce (Figure 2.11).

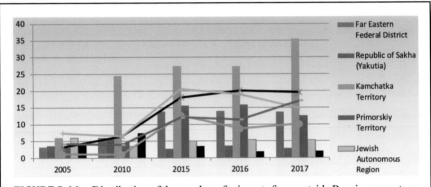

FIGURE 2.11   Distribution of the number of migrants from outside Russia, percentage of the total number of migrants.[21]

The leading region in attracting foreign migrants is Kamchatka territory; in 2017, their share in the total number of foreign migrants was 35.4% with significant growth trend, same as in the Sakhalin region and Amur region (Figure 2.11). In other constituents of the FEFD, the value of this parameter is lowered. The least attractive regions for foreign migrants are Chukotka Autonomous District and the Republic of Sakha (Yakutia), which is mainly owing to the harsh nature and climate in these territories.

The highest share of internal migrants from other regions of Russia is seen in the Chukotka Autonomous District (82.2% in 2017) (Figure 2.12). The average figure for the FEFD was 35.8% in 2017. The lowest share is in Primorskiy territory (27.4%).

---

21   Compiled by the author on the basis of "Regions of Russia. *Socio-Economic Indicators 2011–2018.*" http://www.gks.ru/bgd/regl/b15_14p/Main.htm (accessed on 9 June 2020).

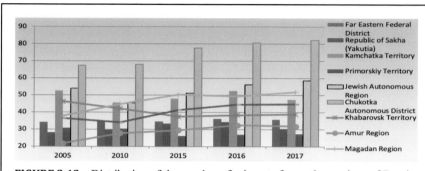

FIGURE 2.12 Distribution of the number of migrants from other regions of Russia, percentage of the total number of migrants.[22]

The interest of foreigners in labor activities grew until 2010 (Figure 2.13). In 2011, changes in Russian migration and labor laws took effect that toughened rules regarding the employment of foreign citizens and introduced limitations for, and even banned some, occupations for foreign migrants.

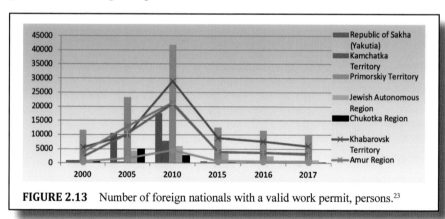

FIGURE 2.13 Number of foreign nationals with a valid work permit, persons.[23]

22. Compiled by the author on the basis of "Regions of Russia. *Socio-Economic Indicators 2011–2018.*" http://www.gks.ru/bgd/regl/b15_14p/Main.htm (accessed on 9 June 2020).
23. Data before 2015 show the number of foreign nationals employed in Russia, while data since 2015 present the number of foreign nationals having a valid work permit. According to the Ministry of Interior of the Russian Federation, this information is monitored since 2011, including foreign nationals who received work permits at the Passport and Visa Center and were not distributed to the Russian Federation's constituents. Data since 2015 are given for foreigners who arrived to Russia with entry visas. "Regions of Russia. *Socio-Economic Indicators-2011–2018.*" http://www.gks.ru/bgd/regl/b15_14p/Main.htm (accessed on 9 June 2020).

The issue regarding whether it is possible to replace Russian citizens employed in the Russian Far East with foreign migrants is addressed frequently enough. Numerous regional development projects suppose the employment of foreign migrants in the FEFD. However, an analysis of the ratio of officially registered foreign employees with the average annual number of employed shows a highly insignificant share of the first (Figure 2.14).

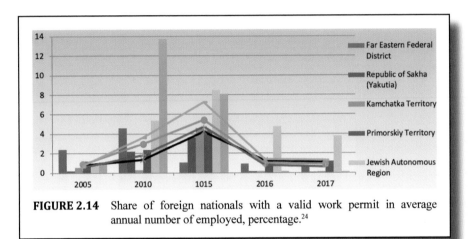

FIGURE 2.14   Share of foreign nationals with a valid work permit in average annual number of employed, percentage.[24]

The highest value of this indicator in the studied period was observed in the Chukotka Autonomous District in 2010 (13.7%); however, in 2017 this figure in these constituents fell to 0.1%. In 2017, the average figure for the FEFD was less than 1% (0.77%). The abrupt decrease in the share of foreign employees coincides with the overall reduction in number of such employees in the FEFD.

The analysis of these figures shows the low attractiveness of the region both for its residents and foreign migrant workers. The living standards and wages in foreign countries that traditionally supplied the labor force to the Far Eastern region considerably increased; therefore,

24. Compiled by the author on the basis of "Regions of Russia. *Socio-Economic Indicators 2011–2018.*" http://www.gks.ru/bgd/regl/b15_14p/Main.htm (accessed on 9 June 2020).

the conditions that were attractive for them in the past do not meet present requirements.

The fear that foreign migrants would fill workplaces and result in massive unemployment among local residents, as well as the general economic and social situation in the Russian Far East, resulted in the formation of the conditions that created a major shortage of labor resources in the region, thus heavily impeding the development of the concerned territory.

In the eight studied years, the make-up of new migrants (by nationality) to the region radically changed. In 2008, the share of Russian nationals was 77.0%, while the share of foreign nationals was 21.6%. The highest number of fellow countrymen arrived in the Republic of Sakha (Yakutia) at 98%, while the minimum arrived in Kamchatka territory (45.6%). In 2017, the share of RF nationals was only 17.1%, while the share of foreigners was 82.4%. The highest number of RF nationals was reported in the Chukotka Autonomous District (62.9%), while the lowest one was seen in Kamchatka territory (6.5%).

Parallel to the inflow of the population to the FEFD, there is an outflow of the population from the region. Outward migration flow from the FEFD may be classified into three sources:

1. Migration of the population to other constituents of the FEFD;
2. Migration of the population beyond FEFD to other constituents of the Russian Federation;
3. Migration of the population to foreign countries.

The dynamics of the number of emigrants from the FEFD is shown in Figure 2.15.

Primorskiy territory and Khabarovsk territory are both the main attraction areas for immigrants and regions of active emigration. In 2008, Primorskiy territory accounted for 22.7% of total migration outflow; the Republic of Sakha (Yakutia) for 21.2%; and Khabarovsk territory for 17.9%. In 2017, Primorskiy territory accounted for

29.7% of emigrants, with Khabarovsk territory accounting for 21.6% and the Republic of Sakha (Yakutia) for only 16.6%. Internal migration (to other regions in Russia) was mainly from Khabarovsk and Primorskiy territories (19.8 and 28.9%, respectively, in 2017) and the Republic of Sakha (Yakutia) (18.2%). The lowest migration outflow was seen in the Chukotka Autonomous District (2.0%). The steep emigration growth in years 2010–2013 then changed to stable annual emigration.

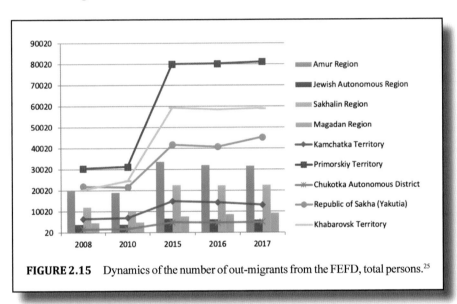

FIGURE 2.15   Dynamics of the number of out-migrants from the FEFD, total persons.[25]

People also continuously migrate across the region. The leader in intra-regional emigration is Primorskiy territory. In 2017, its share in intra-regional emigration was 35.0% which is twice as more than in the second-highest emigration leader (Khabarovsk territory). A considerable share of emigrants leave the FEFD to other constituents of the Russian Federation, making 42.5% of total migration outflow

25. Compiled by the author on the basis of data from the statistical compendium *"Population Size and Migration in the Russian Federation for Years 2009–2016."* http://www.gks.ru (accessed on 9 June 2020).

in 2017. The leaders in intra-national emigration are Primorskiy territory and, following by a slight margin, Khabarovsk territory (each 22.1%).

The distribution of the FEFD's emigrating residents among other regions of Russia is not even. The most attractive RF regions for FEFD's emigrants are Central (26%), Siberian (20.2%), Southern (19.6%), and Northern (17.6%) Federal Districts. In 2017, only 10.2% of the total number of emigrants in this period left the FEFD to move abroad, although this figure increased as compared to 2016. This situation was due to changes in the ruble exchange rate and lowered interest of some migrant workers (Chinese and Koreans) for work in Russia.

The dynamics of migration to CIS States was stable and low, but after an aggravation of the crisis in Russia, this changed to the explosive growth of indicators, particularly for Primorskiy, Khabarovsk, and Kamchatka territories. This trend accelerated even more after economic sanctions against Russia were introduced and following ruble devaluation. These factors mainly influenced the dynamics of emigration beyond Russia, too, except to CIS states. A minor decrease in 2014 changed again to growth in 2017. One of the reasons for this was the toughening of migration laws and the cut-down of quotas to attract a foreign workforce. After the expiry of concluded employment contracts, foreigners return to their countries of origin.

The analysis of dynamics and age structure of emigrants showed differently directed trends in various constituents of the FEFD, as well as violent fluctuations. In average by region, the share of working-age people who emigrated from the FEFD varied between 70 and 80%. The lowest share of the working-age population emigrating from the region was seen in the Magadan region. This was due to the fact that people who have worked in this constituent of the FEFD and earned some money leave to reside in more favorable climatic conditions. Violent fluctuations of the indicator in the Amur region show the reverse trend in the number of arrivals to the region, i.e., people who come to the region tend to leave the region after some defined period. The decrease of the figure in 2010 in all regions shows the reaction of the population to the crisis that suspended any migration both out and into the region. The highest share of working-age emigrants is reported in Primorskiy and Khabarovsk territories, and the Republic of Sakha (Yakutia). In 2017, this figure fell considerably in the first two regions. The growth in the share of working-age individuals among emigrants from the region is seen in the Amur region.

Dynamics of the share of working-age individuals who migrated from the FEFD to RF regions shows a high share of such individuals in the Jewish Autonomous region and Chukotka Autonomous district. Low figures for Magadan region and Kamchatka territory show the dynamics of migration of the above working-age population to the territory with more favorable climate and environmental conditions.

The share of the working-age population among those who emigrated abroad shows an increase, amounting to 74.8% in 2017. The lowest share was reported in the Magadan region (69.0%), with the highest share in the Republic of Sakha (Yakutia) (77.0%). Sharp fluctuations of this rate were reported in turn in every FEFD constituent. The high percentage of this rate corresponds to the share of the population with higher education migrating to the constituents of the region. As this migration is temporary and is due to employment, working-age employees come to the region from abroad and, upon the termination of their contracts, they leave the region still in the working-age range and without unemployable dependents.

The growth in the number of persons with higher education who migrated from the region from 2008 to 2010–2011 was then inverted, which returned figures to the level of 2008. In 2017, the share of persons with higher education who migrated from the FEFD was 27.6%. The lowest share of individuals among the 14+ age group was reported in the Jewish Autonomous region (23.4% in 2017). The highest share was reported in Kamchatka territory (37.8% in 2011) and Khabarovsk territory (35.3% in 2010). In 2017, the highest share was in the Chukotka Autonomous District (34.1%).

The share of persons with general secondary education in the 14+ age group who migrated from the FEFD follows a downward trend. The leading constituent by this parameter in 2017 was the Republic of Sakha (Yakutia) (31.6%), with Kamchatka territory being the last with 13.5%. This situation is due to the growing demand of local employers for workers with this education level, which reduces interest in leaving the region.

The nationality pattern of individuals migrating from the region radically changed in the observed period. In 2008, the highest number of emigrants from the FEFD was RF nationals (98.3%), with non-national residents making 0.8, including CIS nationals (0.7%). The highest share of the RF nationals migrated from Khabarovsk territory (99.4%), with the highest number of foreign nationals migrating from Sakhalin region (2.1%).

In 2017, among people leaving the region, non-RF nationals prevailed at 86.4% (59.6% from CIS states and 40.4% from other countries). The highest share of the RF nationals migrated from Jewish Autonomous region at 34.6%, while the highest number of non-RF nationals migrated from Kamchatka territory at 97.9% (99.6% from CIS states). This situation was due to the economic situation in the country and region, and the current regional policy.

Notwithstanding a great number of arguments for attracting foreign employees to the region, there are arguments against this as well. One of the arguments is that these employees are competitors for RF nationals, and this is an unemployment growth factor. However, one must note that foreign nationals were invited within established entry quotas which helped to more strictly regulate migration flows. The law "On ADTs" enabled employers doing their business within ADTs to employ working migrants without quota limitations, by the nature of their future commercial activities. When using quotas, in order to get a permit to invite a foreign employee, an employer must first prove that it cannot find a required employee in the internal labor market.

Thus, it can be concluded that the FEFD is hardly attractive for the migrant workforce, and proposals made by the RF government to engage a workforce from outside the region can hardly be implemented.

For an employer, a foreign workforce is cheaper, more productive, and less protected by the law. Although, in order for a foreign national to work in Russia, an employer must get a permit to recruit a foreign workforce and pay a state duty. A foreigner has to have a paid medical examination and provide a qualification certificate. Moreover, a migrant worker is to pass a test on the Russian language, and the history and fundamentals of RF laws. If any inspection of an enterprise finds any violations of migration laws, an employee has to pay penalty sanctions.

According to N. N. Deyeva, "Covering the growing workforce demand of the region in the industry sectors that do not require skilled employees stipulates the recruitment of more than 48 thousand foreign workers to the region. In the opinion of experts, only 30% foreign migrant workers work on license, thus official statistics on the use of the foreign migrant workforce in the Russian Far East are underestimated.

Foreigners generally occupy the niches in the labor market where vacancies with heavy and hazardous labor conditions were not sought after by local workers.

The Russian Far East invites working migrants from China, Democratic Peoples' Republic of Korea, Vietnam, and CIS states (mainly in the southern regions of the Far East); most working immigrants are from China.

The foreign workforce is used in construction, catering, retail trade, agriculture, and production sectors. The number of foreign nationals in the employment market of the Russian Far East will grow. If we are to solve the task of ensuring accelerated economic growth of the region, which requires an improvement in the stability of Russia in the Asia Pacific Region, there is no alternative."[26]

The analysis of the components of quality of life and migration in the region will identify objective preconditions of the negative dynamics in employment level and changes in its structure. The region loses a highly skilled workforce that is not satisfied with the relatively low quality of life in the FEFD as compared to other regions of the Russian Federation and with the level available to people who have a similar professional status but reside and work in other regions of the country. This is confirmed by results of the migration analysis conducted.

2.5 WORKFORCE IN THE DIGITAL ECONOMY

The FEFD's labor resources are integrated into the digital economy of Russia and the world. This provides them with a number of competitive strengths and lowers the threat of remoteness from global centers of culture, education, etc.

The analysis of workforce development in the FEFD's digital economy is based on the study of the following indicators:[27]

- Share of households having personal computers in the total number of households, % (personal computers in households);

26. Deyeva, N. N. *Problem of Personnel Shortage in the Russian Far East*, http://www.be5. biz/ekonomika1/r2012/3205.htm (accessed on 9 June 2020); Galetskiy, V. F. *The Russian Far East: Looking for a Demographic Development Strategy*. http://ecfor.ru/wp-content/ uploads/2006/fp/6/11.pdf (accessed on 9 June 2020); Bystritskiy, S. P., & Zausayev, V. K. *The Russian Far East: Demographic Challenges and Chinese Factor*. http://www. iep.ru/files/text/confer/2006_03_20/zausaev_ru.pdf (accessed on 9 June 2020).
27. Sabelnikova, M. A., Abdrakhmanova, G. I., Gokhberg, L. M., Dudorova, O. Y., et al., (2018). *Information Society: Key Characteristics of Constituents of the Russian Federation: Statistical Compendium* (p.216). RF Federal Service of State Statistics, National Research University 'Higher School of Economics,' Moscow: NIU VShE. http://www.gks.ru/free_ doc/doc_2018/info-ob_reg2018.pdf (accessed on 9 June 2020).

- Share of households with Internet access from mobile devices (mobile phones or smartphones, e-book readers, etc.) in the total number of households, % (mobile Internet in households);
- Share of households with broadband Internet in the total number of households, % (broadband Internet in households);
- Share of population that have ever used Internet in the total population aged 15–74 years, % (Internet users);
- Share of population that uses Internet practically every day, in the total population aged 15–74 years, %, (go online every day);
- Share of population that uses mobile devices to go online, in the total population aged 15–74 years, % (go online from mobile devices);
- Share of population that goes online to buy goods and services in the total population aged 15–74 years, % (do shopping online);
- Share of population that goes online to receive public and municipal services in electronic form, in the total population aged 15–72 years who receive public and municipal services, % (receive electronic public services);
- Share of organizations that use internet for internal or external recruitment of personnel, in the total number of organizations, % (online personnel recruitment);
- Share of organizations that use Internet for professional training of their personnel in the total number of organizations, % (online personnel training).

On the whole, the integration of the Russian Far East's workforce equals the average national level, although by mobile Internet and use hereof local users exceed the average national level and take the top position among all regions.

The analysis of the FEFD's constituents in 2017 showed (Figure 2.16) that the least coverage of broadband Internet is in the Chukotka Autonomous District (33.8%) and the Magadan region (59.6%), which is due to the complex climate and environmental conditions, and a population density that is too low for the profitability of Internet network deployment. Nevertheless, Internet is actively used in online personnel training (55% in the Chukotka Autonomous District). The leaders in online shopping are residents of Kamchatka territory (43.8%), while the workforce in the Republic of Sakha (Yakutia) most frequently goes online every day (77.7%). Online personnel recruitment is the most commonly used in the Sakhalin region (37.7%).

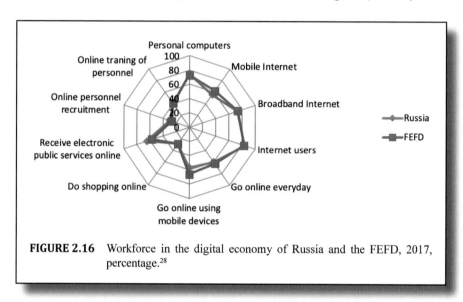

FIGURE 2.16   Workforce in the digital economy of Russia and the FEFD, 2017, percentage.[28]

The FEFD's digital economy develops at Russian-average rates. However, for this region the distribution of information and communication technologies (ICT) and the development of digital competences in the population enable the mitigation of a number of traditional limitations related to remoteness from central regions of the Russian Federation and from developed world economies (Figure 2.17).

28. Compiled by the author on the basis of data from: Sabelnikova, M. A., Abdrakhmanova, G. I., Gokhberg, L. M., Dudorova, O. Y., et al., (2018). *Information Society: Key Characteristics of Constituents of the Russian Federation: Statistical Compendium* (p. 216). RF Federal Service of State Statistics, National Research University 'Higher School of Economics,' Moscow: NIU VShE. http://www.gks.ru/free_doc/doc_2018/info-ob_reg2018.pdf (accessed on 9 June 2020).

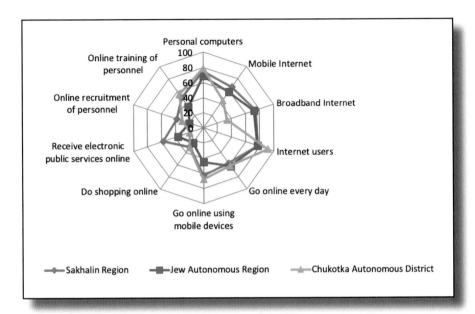

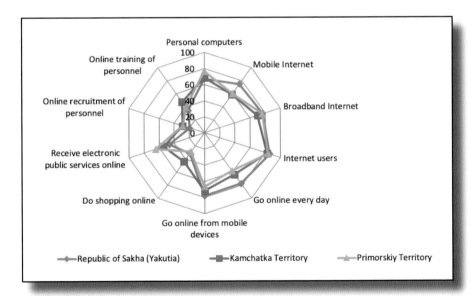

FIGURE 2.17 *(Continued)*

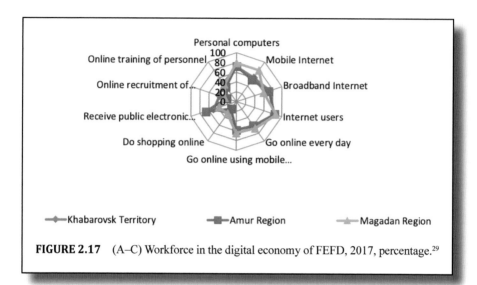

FIGURE 2.17 (A–C) Workforce in the digital economy of FEFD, 2017, percentage.[29]

KEYWORDS

> ➢ **commonwealth of independent states**
> ➢ **digital economy**
> ➢ **educational potential**
> ➢ **Far Eastern Federal District**
> ➢ **labor resource dynamics**
> ➢ **population migration**

---

29. Compiled by the author on the basis of data from: Sabelnikova, M. A., Abdrakhmanova, G. I., Gokhberg, L. M., Dudorova, O. Y., et al., (2018). *Information Society: Key Characteristics of Constituents of the Russian Federation: Statistical Compendium* (p. 216). RF Federal Service of State Statistics, National Research University 'Higher School of Economics,' Moscow: NIU VShE. http://www.gks.ru/free_doc/doc_2018/info-ob_reg2018.pdf (accessed on 9 June 2020).

3 | Priorities to Increase the Workforce in the Russian Far East

3.1 EARNED INCOME OF RESIDENTS IN THE REGION

One of the factors for increasing the region's attraction for residence is the population's economical motivation. The history of the Far Eastern wage supplements begins from the Decree of the USSR Council of Ministers dated August 25, 1946, which is titled "On the Increase in Wages and Salaries, and the Construction of Residential Housing for Workers, Technicians, and Engineers Employed at Enterprises and Construction Projects in the Urals, Siberia, and in the Far East." This decree stated the following: "In view of the fact that severe climatic conditions in the regions of the Urals, Siberia, and the Far East create additional difficulties for workers, technicians, and engineers engaged in heavy labor in the production of coal, ore, oil, and in the metallurgic industry, construction, and load-handling operations—the USSR Council of Ministers considers it necessary to: (a) increase, against the existing rates, wages, and salaries for the above-specified workers, technicians, and engineers, and (b) considerably expand the program of residential construction in the Urals, Siberia, and the Far East, in priority, for workers, technicians, and engineers engaged in heavy labor."

In 1954, following the visit of Nikita S. Khrushchev to Vladivostok, the Russian Far East wage supplement was canceled; however, it returned in four years.[1]

---

1. Two visits of Nikita, S. Khrushchev to Vladivostok, Filatov Yu, Utro Rossii, (2009).

In 1967, by decree of the USSR Council of Ministers dated November 10, 1967, No. 1032, the following decision was made:

1. To approve the size of regional pay factors to the wages and salaries of workers and office employees of enterprises, organizations, and institutions of consumer and food-processing industries, education, health care, housing, and communal services, science, culture, and other sectors of national economy located in the districts of the Far East, Chita region, Buryat ASSR, and the European North, for which these pay factors are not set presently, according to the Annex.

2. The introduction of regional pay factors does not create new rates and position salaries. Regional pay factors shall be applied to wages and salaries without allowance for long-service awards and personal bonuses.

Regional pay factors shall be applied to wages and salaries not exceeding 300 rubles per month. If wages and salaries exceed this amount, pay factors shall be applied to their part equal to 300 rubles.

The Decree of the USSR State Committee for Labor and All-Union Central Soviet of Trade Unions of November 20, 1967, No. 512/П-28, "On the Amount of Regional Pay Factors to Wages and Salaries of Workers and Office Employees of Enterprises, Organizations, and Institutions Located in the Districts of the Far East, Chita Region, Buryat ASSR, and the European North, for which These Pay Factors Have Not Been Set Presently and on Procedure of Their Use" set a 1.20 pay factor for Khabarovsk territory, Primorskiy territory, and Amur region.

The Decree of the Central Committee of CPSU, the USSR Council of Ministers, All-union Central Soviet of Trade Unions of September 4, 1986, No. 53, "On the Introduction of Supplements to Wages and Salaries of Workers and Office Employees of Enterprises, Institutions, and Organizations Located in the Southern Districts of the Far East,

Buryat ASSR, and Chita Region" introduced percentage increments to wages and salaries of workers and office employees for continuous service at enterprises, institutions, and organizations located in the Southern districts of the Russian Far East as follows: 10% after serving one year, with 10% increase every two years of service, but not more than 30% of wages and salaries.

For the youth (aged under 30 years) who have resided in the southern districts of the Russian Far East for at least one year and are employed for the first time, the percentage increment to wages and salaries shall be set in an accelerated manner, namely: 10% increment per each half-year of employment according to subparagraph "e" of paragraph 1 of the Decree of the RSFSR Council of Ministers dated October 22, 1990, No. 458. In addition, according to "Decree of the Council of Ministers of the RF Government dated October 7, 1993, No. 1012," the service record in the above localities entitling workers to receive percentage increments to wages and salaries is totaled independently of the duration of work suspension and the motives of employment termination.

Regional pay factor and percentage increment to wages and salaries are compensation payments for work in localities with special climatic conditions, therefore they shall be paid at the place of actual employment in the amount not less than it is stipulated by the effective laws, i.e., regional pay factor not less than 20% independent of service record, and percentage increment to wages and salaries not less than 30% depending on the duration of employment in the Southern districts of the Far East, notwithstanding the ownership form of an employer.

The mechanism to attract a workforce to the Russian Far East in the administrative-command system period with centralized planning and distribution of funds gave the desired effects, since residents of the Russian Far East actually received a larger income as compared to other regions. Centralized pricing redistributed the high labor costs to the goods manufactured in other regions, thus not lowering the competitive strengths of the goods manufactured in the Russian Far East and increasing their affordability for local residents; the high labor cost neither provoked losses in regional enterprises, nor was neutralized with high prices for goods and services.

Transferring the experience of Far Eastern guarantees (i.e., setting regional pay factors and percentage wage increments) onto the contemporary economy—only in terms of the mandatory setting of wage increments not at the State's expense but from the financial resources of private enterprises—leads to negative phenomena in the economy.

An employer, fulfilling requirements of the State for setting the Far Eastern wage increment and regional pay factor, has to increase its salary budget by 50% (30% and 20%). Therefore, private organizations fulfill state guarantees at their cost and expense, and specifically, at the expense of consumers, who are mostly Far Easterners who have to buy expensive products. Moreover, these supplements (that were designed and adopted as a stimulating element for people who reside and have their business in the Russian Far East) are liable to taxation: a 13% income tax for individuals and about 30% in social taxes. The amount of the latter is included in the product cost and increases its price. In addition, for every 1000 rubles of an employee's salary, the Far Eastern wage increment (20%), or 200 rubles, and regional pay factor (30%), or 300 rubles, are paid. Thus, the salary budget per 1000 rubles of a Far Easterner's salary is equal to $1000 + 200 + 300 = 1500$ rubles. The "State guarantee" is $200+300=500$ Rubles. Moreover, personal income tax (13%) is 195 rubles (65 rubles out of the 500 rubles' guarantee). Social payments (30%) are 450 rubles (150 rubles out of 500 rubles' guarantee). As a result, the labor price "encumbered" with the Far Eastern guarantee equals $1500 + 450 = 1950$ rubles ($500 + 150 = 650$ rubles out of the 500 rubles' guarantee). Moreover, the labor price without the "State guarantee" is 1300 rubles. Total payments to the State are $195 + 450 = 645$ rubles ($65 + 150 = 215$ rubles out of the 500 rubles' guarantee).

Thus, "compensatory" stimulating payments guaranteed by the State according to the laws provide larger gain to the State (645 rubles) than to an employee (500 rubles).

Having paid personal income tax (which includes this guarantee) an employee will pay it again by buying Far Eastern products that contain the price of labor together with the calculated guarantee and social payments increased by the guarantee's amount. If an employer did not pay the "State guarantee" and the tax on this State guarantee, the price of labor to be included in the product cost would be 33% less. An employee who receives the Far Eastern allowance in an amount of about 50% will pay the 13% tax to the State on it and pay an extra 33% for goods and services; thus, the "real" stimulating allowance is just 4%. Taking into account climate specifics, a weak infrastructure base, environmental problems, and permanent threats related to the near-border location of the region, this allowance percentage cannot be an effective stimulus both for retention and attraction to the region's workforce capable of ensuring economic growth.

The basic document that regulates the provision of Far Eastern guarantees is the RF Labor Code adopted in 2001. Chapter 50 is fully devoted to guarantees provided to residents of the northern regions of Russia, including regions of the Russian Far East. This chapter determines regional pay factor, percentage wage increments, additional day-offs, shortened working weeks, annual paid leave, guarantees for medical services, compensation for travel expenses (plus luggage charges) to the leave location and back, and compensation for resettlement expenses.

Presently, regional pay factor is applied to the following payments:

- Wages and salaries since the moment of taking the job position;
- Set of wage supplements, including sums stipulated for continuous service (so-called continuous service period);
- Allowances fixed by effective provisions for remuneration rates (categories) as well as for academic degrees, high skill, and qualification level;

- Compensations designed to compensate an employee for hazardous and dangerous working conditions (this category includes night work conditions);
- Annual remuneration to be paid according to an employee's performance ("thirteenth-month pay");
- Payments for seasonal labor and for temporary employment;
- Payments in case of temporary disability ("sick leaves");
- Payment to employees holding multiple jobs (part-time employees);
- Minimum legal wage.
- Regional pay factor shall not be applied in the calculation of:
- Leave allowance;
- Remuneration and financial aid if those are paid in the form of a one-off bonus and not provided under the terms and conditions of an employment contract (i.e., granted on the employer's initiative);
- Northern allowances.

The effect of a regional pay factor extends to pensions and allowances only as long as an individual resides in this region. Should an individual relocate to a more favorable place of residence, the allowance will be reduced (or fully canceled).

The northern allowance will be accrued in full if an employee took employment at an enterprise before the age of thirty years and after January 2005, but only provided that s/he had previously lived in any region of the Far North for not less than five years (counting until December 31, 2004). If an individual had lived in a Far North region for less than five years, but for more than one year, the northern allowance shall be applied in an accelerated mode: for regions of the Far North after the first six months of employment, 20% allowance is provided and further allowance is increased by 20% every half-year, until 60% is achieved. Afterwards the allowance will be increased by

20% per year of service, but not higher than the fixed standard rate. For localities equated to regions of the Far North, the 10% increment is stipulated every half-year.

The amount of northern allowances in every constituent of the Far Eastern Federal District (FEFD) varies (Table 3.1).[2] The author proposes some variants for using Far Eastern guarantees.

TABLE 3.1   Amount of Northern Allowance and Regional Pay Factors in the FEFD[3]

Region	Northern Allowance Range, Percentage	Regional Pay Factor, Percentage
Amur Region	30 to 50	1.3
Jewish Autonomous Region	30	1.2
Kamchatka Territory	80 to 100	1.6 to 2
Magadan Region	80 to 100	1.7
Primorskiy Territory	30 to 100	1.2 to 1.4
Republic of Sakha (Yakutia)	80 to 100	1.4 to 2
Sakhalin Region	50 to 100	1.4 to 2
Khabarovsk Territory	30 to 100	1.2 to 1.6
Chukotka Autonomous District	100	2

The first variant stipulates exempting from personal income taxes the sums that employers pay to employees pursuant to requirements of the State. These amounts are guaranteed by the State according to laws, but are provided by an employer to its employees as a compensation for living in severe climatic conditions. Under this variant, the national budget will be short of tax income.

If we take Russian statistics data as a basis, we may calculate the amount of short-received money, on one hand, and the reduction of the burden on the business, on the other. The negative effect from a short-term perspective at the initial stage of introduction of this proposal

2.   Novikova, I. V., (2016). Prospects of using Far Eastern guarantees as an instrument for promoting employment in the region. *Living Standards in the Regions of Russia, 220,* 206–219.
3.   Compiled by the author.

will be that the state budget will be short of tax income. However, in the long-term, this situation will change because of production growth and an increase in employment level and, therefore, the growth of gross regional product. Employees will be interested in getting the official salary, a part of which will not be subject to tax. Besides, state expenses to support the unemployed will be reduced, since households' increased demand will stimulate production growth and, therefore, demand for the workforce.

The second variant of changes for using Far Eastern guarantees stipulates full exemption from taxing the amounts of the Far Eastern guarantee. In this case, the State will not get the 13% personal income tax and 30% social taxes.

The third variant involves transferring the financing of State guarantees to federal budget expenditures. In this case, the State receives less tax income than due, and approaches significant expenses.

The fourth variant stipulates the provision of State guarantees out of budget funds only for individuals employed in top-priority industry sectors that have strategic importance because of social significance or because they may become growth points and creates a multiplicative effect for the whole region's development.

The fifth variant is directed toward the provision of State guarantees only to firms registered as legal entities of the FEFD.

The companies that are geographically located in the region, but are registered in other regions provide guarantees to their employees and pay their taxes by themselves. This will stimulate the registration of companies at their place of business and prevent transfer of taxes to other regions. Employees, too, will be interested to be employed in the region's enterprises.

Joint ventures with the participation of foreign capital or foreign companies provide guarantees at their own expense. In this case, the State may provide them with benefits for taxing these amounts, if these entities operate in priority sectors.

According to the laws of the Russian Federation, Far Eastern guarantees shall be provided to all individuals employed in this territory, irrespective of their nationality. For the support of Russian employees, the State could assume-guarantee provision and tax exemption expenses. An employer recruiting a foreign workforce will have to bear the relative expenditures on its own.

An important condition of implementing proposed variants is funding all apparent and non-apparent expenditures out of the federal budget; otherwise, they are senseless because the burden of the guarantee passes over again to Far Easterners. The introduction of these variants will contribute to a real support to economic growth, solving depopulation problems and improving the quality of life in the region.

3.2 DEVELOPMENT OF SMALL BUSINESSES AND SELF-EMPLOYMENT

One of the factors motivating a population increase in the region is the development opportunity of small business and self-employment. The FEFD has a significant potential for developing this type of employment, including using international relations.

The number of small businesses in the region is gradually growing (Figure 3.1). The maximum development of small businesses was reported in Primorskiy territory and Khabarovsk territory, where in the seven-year review period the number of small businesses (including micro-enterprises) grew by 1.5 times. The Territorial Business Support Agency and Small Business Support Fund operate in the Khabarovsk territory. In Primorskiy territory, small businesses are supported by the Business Development Center and Business Support Center. Small businesses are least developed in the Chukotka Autonomous district and Jewish Autonomous region. There the share of micro-enterprises among small businesses is highest and gradually increases (Figure 3.2).

The highest share of micro-enterprises is in Kamchatka and Primorskiy territories (95%), while the lowest one is in the Jewish Autonomous region (86.4%).

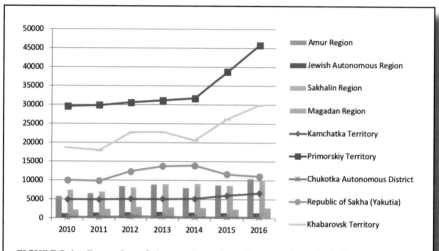

FIGURE 3.1   Dynamics of the number of small enterprises (including microenterprises) in the FEFD (by end of year).[4]

---

4. Number of medium enterprises is the number of economic entities belonging to medium businesses active as of the end of the reporting year, i.e. legal entities employing 101 to 250 individuals, with proceeds from sales of goods (work, services) for the previous year (without VAT) to be not more than 2 billion rubles. Number of small enterprises is the number of economic entities active as of the end of the reporting year and belonging to small businesses (including those that suspend their commercial activities for not more than 2 years), i.e. legal entities employing up to 100 individuals (inclusive), with proceeds from sales of goods (work, services) for the previous year (without VAT) to be not more than 800 million rubles. Number of micro-enterprises is the number of economic entities active as of the end of the reporting year and belonging to small businesses is the number of economic entities active as of the end of the reporting year and belonging to small businesses (including those that suspend their commercial activities for not more than 2 years), i.e. legal entities employing in average up to 15 individuals (inclusive), with income for the previous year to be not more than 120 million rubles. Compiled by the author on the basis of Small and medium-scale enterprises in Russia 2015, 2017. http://www.gks.ru/bgd/regl/b17_47/Main.htm (accessed on 9 June 2020).

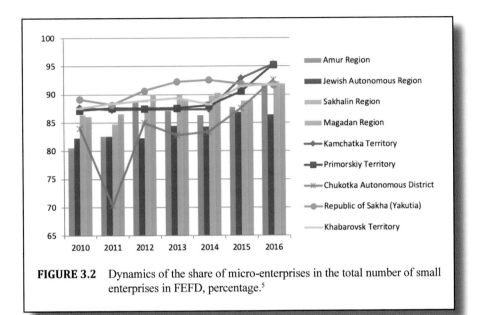

FIGURE 3.2 Dynamics of the share of micro-enterprises in the total number of small enterprises in FEFD, percentage.[5]

In the FEFD, numerous measures are being taken to stimulate the development of small business and self-employment set forth in the "Development Strategy of Small and Medium Businesses in the Russian Federation for the Period Until 2030,"[6] including:

- Reduction of a tax rate for enterprises that apply a simplified taxation system;
- Tax holiday for newly registered individual entrepreneurs engaged in certain economic activities and using a simplified taxation system;
- Subsidies and financial support;
- Professional training and consulting.

5. Compiled by the author on the basis of small and medium-sized enterprises entrepreneurship in Russia 2015, 2017. http://www.gks.ru/bgd/regl/b17_47/Main.htm (accessed on 9 June 2020).
6. *Directive of the RF Government*, (2016). No. 1083.

The major portion of small enterprises is in wholesale and retail trade, car, and motorcycle repair, household goods, and personal items (over 36%). Over 19% of small enterprises deal with transactions with real estate property, hiring, and leasing, and the provision of services. Small businesses in research and development (R&D) make up less than 1%.

This structure mirrors the overall structure of the manufacturing sector in the Far Eastern region. This structure is stable enough, with considerable growth only in the share of transport and communication enterprises (by 16%), which is related with growing demand for these services (Figures 3.3 and 3.4).

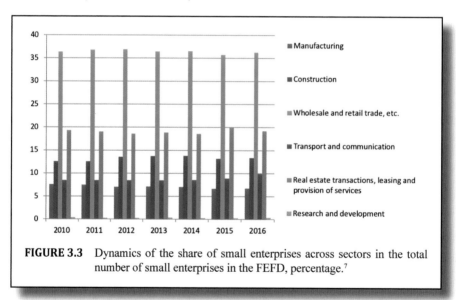

FIGURE 3.3 Dynamics of the share of small enterprises across sectors in the total number of small enterprises in the FEFD, percentage.[7]

The dynamics of the share of micro-enterprises across sectors fully coincide with the dynamics of the share of small enterprises, of which the first ones are included. The dynamics of small enterprise development in specific sectors is shown in Figures 3.5 and 3.6.

7. Compiled by the author on the basis of Small and medium-sized enterprises entrepreneurship in Russia 2015, 2017. http://www.gks.ru/bgd/regl/b17_47/Main.htm (accessed on 9 June 2020).

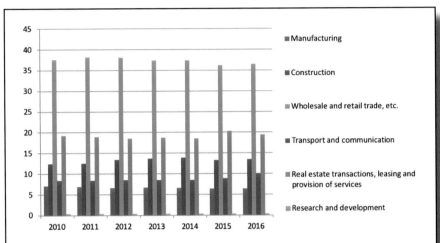

FIGURE 3.4 Dynamics of the share of micro-enterprises across sectors in the total number of micro-enterprises in the FEFD, percentage.[8]

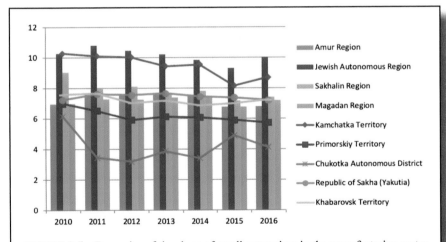

FIGURE 3.5 Dynamics of the share of small enterprises in the manufacturing sector within the total number of small enterprises (including micro-enterprises), percentage.[9]

---

8. *Ibid.*
9. *Ibid.*

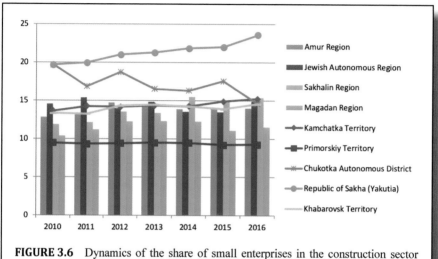

FIGURE 3.6 Dynamics of the share of small enterprises in the construction sector within the total number of small enterprises (including micro-enterprises), percentage.[10]

The share of small manufacturing enterprises in the total number of small enterprises is highest in the Jewish Autonomous region (10% in 2016) and Kamchatka territory (8.7% in 2016), and lowest in the Chukotka Autonomous District (4% in 2016) (Figure 3.7).

The share of small construction enterprises in the total number of small enterprises (including micro-enterprises) is highest in the Republic of Sakha (Yakutia) (23.6%), and lowest in Primorskiy territory (9.3%) and the Magadan region (11.6%).

The significant share of small businesses (including micro-enterprises) is in such sectors as wholesale and retail trade; motor vehicle and motorcycle repair, household goods, and personal items. The share of such enterprises is highest in Primorskiy territory (41.3%) and Khabarovsk territory (38.8%), and lowest in the Republic of Sakha (Yakutia) (22.6%). The significant share of these enterprises corresponds to national small business development dynamics, and the pattern of wide distribution of this business in these constituents of the Russian Federation (Figures 3.8 and 3.9).

---

10. *Ibid*

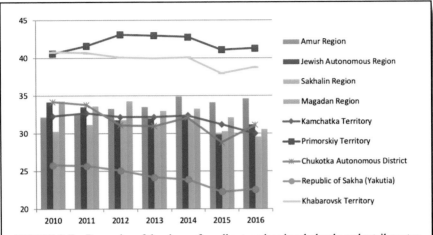

FIGURE 3.7 Dynamics of the share of small enterprises in wholesale and retail, motor vehicle and motorcycle repair, household goods, and personal items in the total number of small enterprises (including micro-enterprises), percentage.[11]

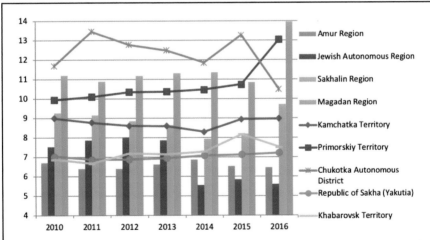

FIGURE 3.8 Dynamics of the share of small enterprises of the transportation and communications sectors in the total number of small enterprises (including micro-enterprises), percentage.[12]

---

11. *Ibid.*
12. Compiled by the author on the basis of Small and medium-sized enterprises entrepreneurship in Russia 2015, 2017. http://www.gks.ru/bgd/regl/b17_47/Main.htm (accessed on 9 June 2020).

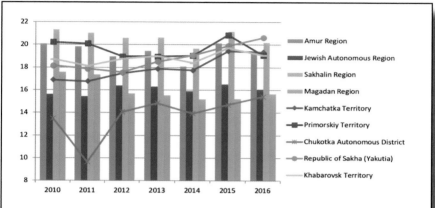

FIGURE 3.9 Dynamics of the share of small enterprises engaged in real estate transactions, leasing, and provision of services in the total number of small enterprises (including micro-enterprises), percentage.[13]

The highest share of small enterprises of the transport and communications sector in the total number of small enterprises from 2010 to 2015 was reported in the Chukotka Autonomous District, but it fell sharply in 2016 (10.5%). The share of such enterprises is significant in the Magadan region (13.9%) and Primorskiy territory (13.0%), with a growth trend reported.

The highest share of small enterprises engaged in real estate transactions, leasing, and provision of services in the total number of small enterprises (including micro-enterprises), was reported in 2016 in the Republic of Sakha (Yakutia) (20.6%), and with the lowest share of those reported in the Chukotka Autonomous District (15.4%) (Figure 3.10).

The share of small enterprises in the FEFED's R&D sector in the total number of small enterprises (including micro-enterprises) is less than 1%, which is a serious factor hampering the development of scientific potential. The highest development potential is in the Chukotka

---

13. *Ibid.*

Autonomous District (0.82%) and the Republic of Sakha (Yakutia) (0.63%), while the lowest one is in the Sakhalin region (0.13%).

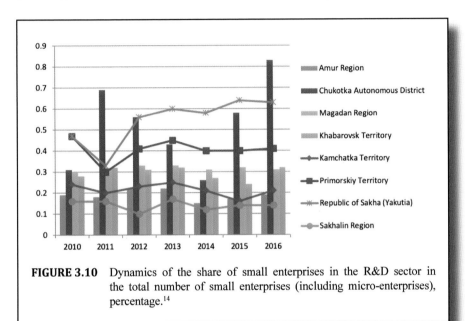

FIGURE 3.10 Dynamics of the share of small enterprises in the R&D sector in the total number of small enterprises (including micro-enterprises), percentage.[14]

The highest average number of employees of small enterprises (including micro-enterprises) was reported in Primorskiy territory (159.6 thousand employees in 2016) and Khabarovsk territory (150.9 thousand employees in 2016), while the lowest number is in the Chukotka Autonomous District (1.6 thousand employees in 2016). The overall employment dynamics remain stable (Figures 3.11 and 3.12).

Active change in dynamics of the average number of employees of micro-enterprises was observed only in Primorskiy territory (75.3 thousand persons) and Khabarovsk territory (45.6 thousand persons). One must note that the number of employees of micro-enterprises in the Khabarovsk Territory decreased, while the number of employees at small enterprises increased (Figures 3.13 and 3.14).

---

14. *Ibid.*

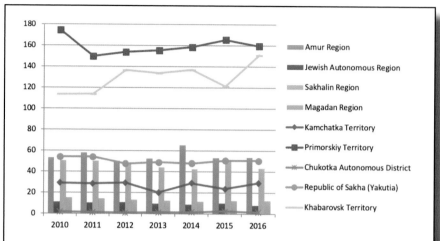

FIGURE 3.11 Dynamics of the average number of employees at small enterprises (including micro-enterprises), thousand persons.[15]

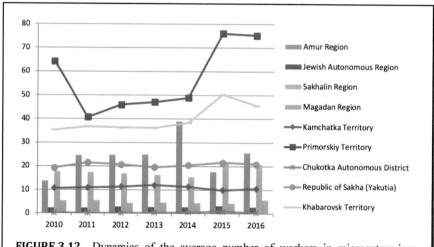

FIGURE 3.12 Dynamics of the average number of workers in microenterprises, thousand persons.[16]

---

15. *Ibid.*
16. Compiled by the author on the basis of Small and medium-sized enterprises entrepreneurship in Russia 2015, 2017. http://www.gks.ru/bgd/regl/b17_47/Main.htm (accessed on 9 June 2020).

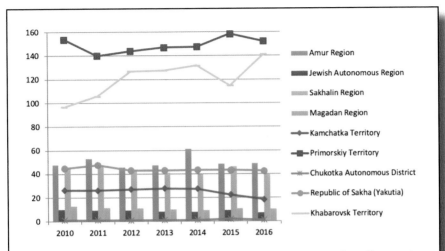

FIGURE 3.13 Dynamics of the average number of employees of small enterprises (exclusive of external part-timers) (including micro-enterprises), thousand persons.[17]

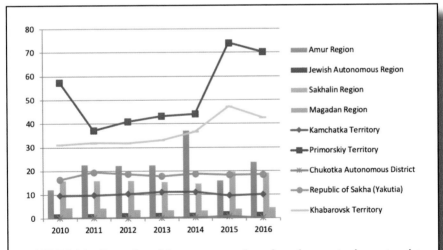

FIGURE 3.14 Dynamics of the average number of employees at micro-enterprises (exclusive of external part-timers), thousand persons.[18]

17. *Ibid.*
18. *Ibid.*

The majority of the employed at small enterprises are employees minus external part-timers (over 90% of the total number of employed at these enterprises). That is, the employees, for whom this employment is primary. The dynamics of the average number of employees of micro-enterprises except for external part-timers fully coincide with the respective dynamics for small enterprises (Figure 3.15).

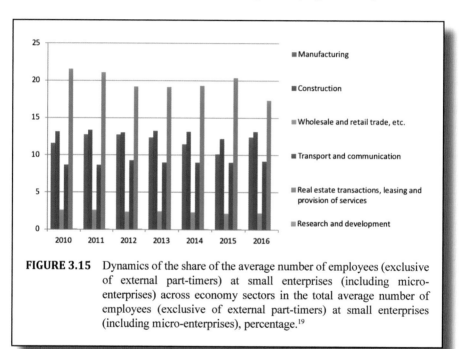

FIGURE 3.15 Dynamics of the share of the average number of employees (exclusive of external part-timers) at small enterprises (including micro-enterprises) across economy sectors in the total average number of employees (exclusive of external part-timers) at small enterprises (including micro-enterprises), percentage.[19]

The greater share of the average number of employees (exclusive of external part-timers) at small enterprises (including micro-enterprises) across economy sectors in the total average number of employees (exclusive of external part-timers) at small enterprises (including micro-enterprises) is observed among enterprises engaged in real estate property operations, leasing, and provision of services, although since 2010 this share has considerably shrunk (from 21.6 to 17.4%). The

19. *Ibid.*

lowest share accounts for the employed in the field of R&D (less than 1%) (Figures 3.16 and 3.17).

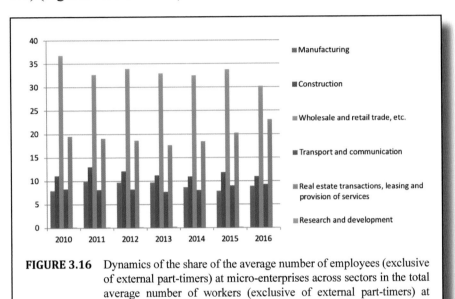

FIGURE 3.16 Dynamics of the share of the average number of employees (exclusive of external part-timers) at micro-enterprises across sectors in the total average number of workers (exclusive of external part-timers) at micro-enterprises, percentage.[20]

The situation at micro-enterprises is considerably different. The highest share of the average number of employees (exclusive of external part-timers) at micro-enterprises across economy sectors in the total average number of employees (exclusive of external part-timers) is observed at enterprises of the wholesale and retail trade sector (30.2% in 2016). However, in 2016 this share considerably decreased at the cost of an increase in the number of the employed at enterprises engaged in real estate property operations, leasing, and provision of services. The lowest share of employees is also in the R&D sector but, in this case, it amounts to 8.3% in 2016 and approximately equals to the share of employees in the manufacturing sector.

---

20. Compiled by the author on the basis of Small and medium-sized enterprises entrepreneurship in Russia 2015, 2017. http://www.gks.ru/bgd/regl/b17_47/Main.htm (accessed on 9 June 2020).

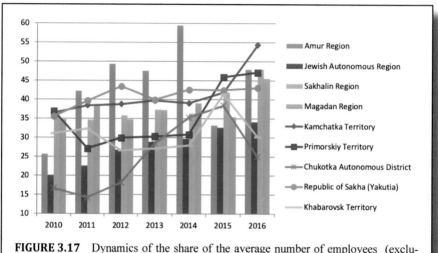

FIGURE 3.17 Dynamics of the share of the average number of employees (exclusive of external part-timers) at micro-enterprises in the total average number of employees (exclusive of external part-timers) at small enterprises (including micro-enterprises), percentage.[21]

The share of the average number of employees (exclusive of external part-timers) at micro-enterprises in the total average number of employees (exclusive of external part-timers) at small enterprises (including micro-enterprises) varies between 25 and 50%. The highest figure is in Kamchatka territory (54.4% in 2016), and the lowest figure is in the Chukotka Autonomous District (25% in 2016). This is a steep decline as compared to 2015 at 38.5% (Figure 3.18).

Employees in the manufacturing sector account for 5 to 22%, with the highest share in the Jewish Autonomous region (22% in 2016), and with the lowest share in the Magadan region (4.8% in 2016) (Figures 3.19 and 3.20).

The share of employed in construction in the observed period fell and in 2016 varied between 7 and 17%: the lowest figure was in the Magadan region (6.7%), while the highest figure was in the Khabarovsk territory and the Republic of Sakha Yakutia (17%).

---

21. *Ibid.*

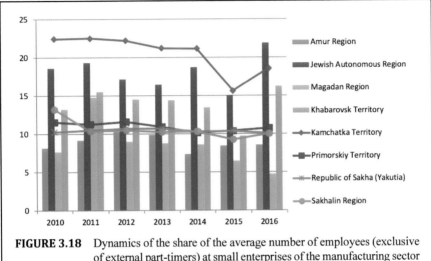

FIGURE 3.18 Dynamics of the share of the average number of employees (exclusive of external part-timers) at small enterprises of the manufacturing sector in the total number of small enterprises (including micro-enterprises), percentage.[22]

The share of the employed in wholesale and retail trade, repair, and maintenance of motor vehicles and motorcycles, household goods and personal items varies between 15 and 45%. The leader by this parameter is the Chukotka Autonomous District (36.4% in 2016), while the lowest figure is in the Jewish Autonomous region (19.2% in 2016) (Figure 3.21).

The share of those employees engaged at transport and communications enterprises varies between 3 and 15%. The highest share is reported in Primorskiy territory and the Magadan region. In 2016, Chukotka Autonomous District showed a zero value of this parameter. Due to the fact that transport infrastructure is sufficiently developed and demand in the sector cannot be fully covered with major enterprises, these parameters may evidence the availability of clandestine employment and activities in this sector.

---

22. Compiled by the author on the basis of Small and medium-sized enterprises entrepreneurship in Russia 2015, 2017. http://www.gks.ru/bgd/regl/b17_47/Main.htm (accessed on 9 June 2020).

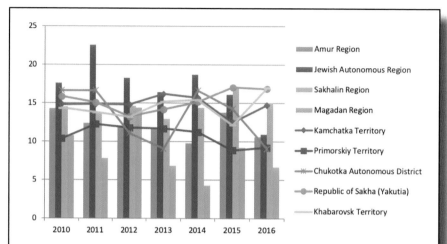

FIGURE 3.19 Dynamics of the share of the average number of employees (exclusive of external part-timers) at small enterprises in the construction sector in the total number of small enterprises (including micro-enterprises), percentage.[23]

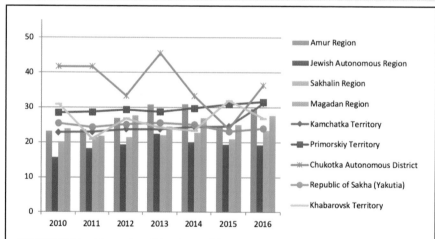

FIGURE 3.20 Dynamics of the share of the average number of employees (exclusive of external part-timers) at small enterprises in the sectors of wholesale and retail, repair, and maintenance of motor vehicles and motorcycles, household goods, and personal items in the total number of small enterprises (including micro-enterprises), percentage.[24]

23. *Ibid.*
24. *Ibid.*

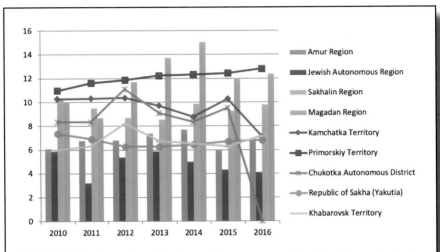

FIGURE 3.21   Dynamics of the share of the average number of employees (exclusive of external part-timers) at small enterprises of the transportation and communications sectors in the total number of small enterprises (including micro-enterprises), percentage.[25]

The share of employed in real estate operations, lease, and service provision varies between 8 and 24%.

2016 saw the growth of this parameter in the Jewish Autonomous region only from 15% in 2015 to 18% in 2016. In this period the share of employees in Kamchatka territory fell half (from 16 to 8%). The highest share of these parameters was reported in Khabarovsk territory (20%) (Figures 3.22 and 3.23).

The number of the employed (including individual entrepreneurs, hired employees, partners, and helping family members) in the individual entrepreneurship sector in 2010–2016 never exceeded 100 thousand persons. The highest figure was reported in Primorskiy territory (91.6 thousand persons in 2016); with the lowest figure reported in the Chukotka Autonomous District (1.5 thousand persons) (Figures 3.24 and 3.25).

---

25. *Ibid.*

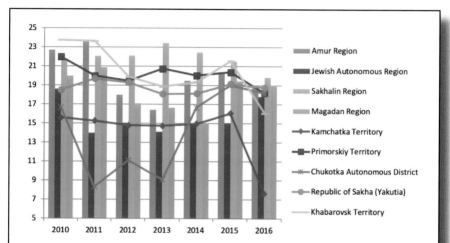

FIGURE 3.22 Dynamics of the share of the average number of employees (exclusive of external part-timers) at small enterprises in the sectors of real estate transactions, leasing, and provision of services in the total number of small enterprises (including micro-enterprises), percentage.[26]

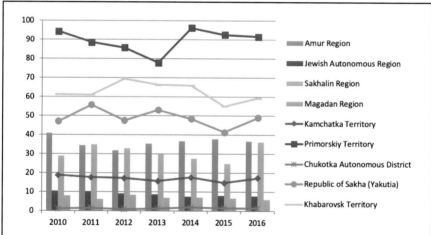

FIGURE 3.23 Dynamics of the number of individuals (including of sole entrepreneurs, hired employees, partners, and helping family members) engaged in sole entrepreneurship sector, thousand persons.[27]

---

26. Compiled by the author on the basis of small and medium-sized enterprises entrepreneurship in Russia 2015, 2017. http://www.gks.ru/bgd/regl/b17_47/Main.htm (accessed on 9 June 2020).

27. *Ibid.*

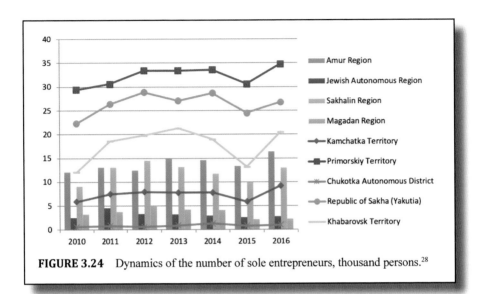

FIGURE 3.24 Dynamics of the number of sole entrepreneurs, thousand persons.[28]

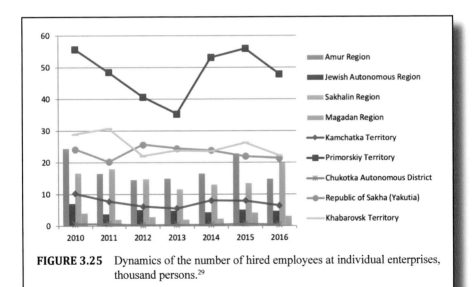

FIGURE 3.25 Dynamics of the number of hired employees at individual enterprises, thousand persons.[29]

28. *Ibid.*

29. Compiled by the author on the basis of small and medium-sized enterprises entrepreneurship in Russia 2015, 2017. http://www.gks.ru/bgd/regl/b17_47/Main.htm (accessed on 9 June 2020).

The number of individual entrepreneurs reached its maximum in 2016, i.e., 35 thousand persons (Primorskiy territory). In 2016, this indicator grew in all regions as compared to 2015.

The number of employees reached its maximum of 56 thousand persons in 2015 (Primorskiy territory). In 2016, this parameter increased only in the Sakhalin region.

The analysis of the development of individual entrepreneurship in the FEFD showed that in the observed period the relevant indicators were stable enough. Certain hikes and falls were due to the implementation in individual regions of pilot projects aimed at supporting small business, and state investments that have priority in support of this sphere. The top constituent in small business development is Primorskiy territory where the highest number of enterprises and employees in the field is reported. The wholesale and retail trade sector contributes significantly to this indicator.

KEYWORDS

> - autonomous region
> - dynamics
> - entrepreneurs
> - micro-enterprises
> - Primorskiy territory
> - research and development

Key Elements of the "Strategy of Workforce Development in the Far Eastern Federal District Until 2035"

The strategizing methodology of V. L. Kvint underlies the concept of the strategy of workforce development in the FEFD until 2035.[1] According to this methodology, the strategy proposed has a certain place in the system of global and regional strategies (Figure 4.1).

FIGURE 4.1 Place of the FEFD's workforce development strategy in the system of global and regional strategies.

1. Kvint, V. L., (2015). *Strategy for the Global Market: Theory and Practical Applications*. New York, London, Routledge-Taylor & Francis; Kvint, V. L., (2019). *Concept of Strategizing*. V.I. St. Petersburg: SZIU RANHiGS, (Library of a Strategic Thinker).

The FEFD's labor force development strategy is an integral part of global, international, national, and regional strategies. The formation of a global employment market on the basis of using information and communication technologies (ICT) allows the workforce to function regardless of its geographical location, i.e., so-called virtual migration is possible.

Labor resources in the Russian Far East have a number of competitive strengths as compared to employees from other countries, as well as to Russian nationals residing in regions to the west. First, the FEFD's territory borders on such developed (including in terms of information) countries as the USA, Japan, Southern Korea, and China. Therefore, there exists an opportunity for permanent migration to those countries or temporary migration to acquire experience and work record. Secondly, Far Eastern employees are always in close contact with employees and employers of Asia Pacific countries, and therefore can communicate with them and are aware of the specifics of the Asian mentality including employment relations. Thirdly, the labor of Far Easterners is relatively cheaper than that of the so-called western employees, and lastly than that of Asian employees. Fourthly, a high unemployment rate and clandestine employment make residents of the Russian Far East leave the region for employment opportunities, therefore the FEFD's employment market, notwithstanding a massive shortage of certain professionals, has an excess of labor supply in certain fields.

The FEFD's workforce development strategy should be integrated into Russia's national development strategy, and into the national workforce development strategy of the Russian Federation. Alignment of these strategies is the requisite condition for the stability and development of the Russian State. Residents of the Russian Far East feel their isolation from the central regions of the country and do not completely identify with them, which creates certain threats both for the region and the whole country.

Other Russian territories regional strategy priorities should also account for the FEFD's workforce development strategy. At the same time, the strategy should also consider these priorities as a potential opportunity for workforce training, development, and promotion.

Any strategy is implemented by corporations by taking their own interests into account. Corporate interests of the Russian Far East are represented in reasonable detail in the monograph *The Russian Far East: Strategic Priorities for Sustainable Development*.[2] Workforce development strategy is directly implemented in corporate strategies. It should be noted that, notwithstanding the threat of displacement of labor resources with information resources, no corporation can exist without labor resources at all. Respectively, the FEFD's workforce development strategy should be aligned with corporate regional strategies.

Personalized strategy is the main priority since in free society an individual builds his or her career and whole life strategy. Therefore, the account of personal interests in the FEFD's Workforce Development Strategy is underlying. Otherwise, this strategy would be effective but not implemented.

4.1 GLOBAL, NATIONAL, AND REGIONAL TRENDS IN WORKFORCE DEVELOPMENT

The workforce of the Russian Far East is influenced by numerous global, national, and regional trends.

---

2. Darkin, S., & Kvint, V., (2016). *The Russian Far East, Strategic Priorities for Sustainable Development*. Canada, Apple Academic Press.

4.1.1   The Green Economy[3]

According to Report V of the International Labor Organization at the International Labor Conference (102nd session, in 2013) "Sustainable Development, Decent Work, and Green Jobs," "modeling undertaken by the International Institute for Labor Studies (IILS) confirms the conclusions of other assessments: that much higher concentrations of GHGs in the atmosphere will increasingly curb economic output and aggregate productivity levels. In particular, the IILS's global economic linkages (GEL) model suggests that productivity levels in 2030 would be 2.4 percent lower than today and 7.2 percent lower by 2050 in a BAU case. Already today, extreme weather events with likely links to climate change are leading to direct losses of jobs and incomes."

"A greener economy could lead to net gains of up to 60 million jobs. These findings are in line with the double-dividend hypothesis, according to which policy measures can achieve economic benefits (in particular employment gains) and environmental improvements at the same time. Much of the additional employment in a greener economy will be created in the production of green goods and services. While evidence is limited, it suggests that these jobs tend to be more qualified, safer, and better paid than comparable jobs in the same or similar sectors."

Thus, in the world there is a long felt need to build the green economy, i.e., environmentally clean economy and, respectively, green jobs. In conditions of a relatively "clean" environmental situation in the Russian Far East, development of a green economy and green jobs may bring a competitive gain to the region.

---

3.   "UNEP defines a green economy as one that results in improved well-being and social equity while significantly reducing environmental risks and ecological scarcities. In its simplest expression, a green economy can be thought as one which is low carbon, resource efficient socially inclusive. In a green economy, growth of employment and incomes are ensured with public and private investments that reduce carbon emissions and pollution, improve efficiency of using energy and resources and prevent loss of biodiversity and ecosystem services." From: UNEP, (2011). *Towards a Green Economy: Path Towards Sustainable Development and Eradication of Poverty* (p. 16). Nairobi.

4.1.2 Decent Jobs

At the 2012 UN Conference for sustainable development (Rio+20) a focus was made on decent work as the prime goal and a driver of sustainable development and a greener economy.[4] The term "decent work" was introduced by the International Labor Organization in June 1999. According to the ILO's approach, the goal of decent work is both the creation of jobs and the creation of affordable quality jobs. For the ILO, decent work underlies social progress and thus became one of the main concepts of contemporary policy. Decent work involves gender issues and includes four main elements:

- Productive and freely chosen employment;
- Right for labor;
- Social protection;
- Social dialogue.[5]

In 2015, world leaders agreed on seventeen goals to achieve a better world by 2030.[6] These goals are aimed at fighting poverty, fighting inequality, and stopping climate change. The eighth goal was to create conditions to ensure decent work. The achievement of this goal involves the following:

- Sustainable economic growth per capita according to national conditions, in particular annual GDP growth of at least 7% in the least developed countries.
- Achievement of higher levels of workforce productivity by means of diversification, renewals, and innovations, including by focusing on the sectors with high added value and labor-consuming sectors.

---

4. Sustainable development, decent work and green jobs, Report V of International Labor Organization at International Labor Conference, Session 102, 2013.
5. Sustainable development, decent work and green jobs, Report V of International Labor Organization at International Labor Conference, Session 102, 2013.
6. https://www.globalgoals.org/8-decent-work-and-economic-growth (accessed on 9 June 2020).

- Support of development-oriented policies that support productive activities, the creation of decent jobs, entrepreneurship, creation, and innovations, and the stimulation of the formalization and growth of micro-, small-, and medium-sized enterprises, including by means of access to financial services.
- The gradual (through 2030) increase of global efficiency in the use of resources in consumption and production sectors, and the creation of conditions to detach economic growth from environmental deterioration according to ten-year framework programs for sustainable consumption and production.
- By 2030 ensuring full and productive employment and decent jobs for all women and men, including youth and reduced mobility groups, and equal payment for equal-quality work.
- Taking prompt and effective measures to eradicate forced labor, modern slavery, and human trafficking, ensure prohibition and eradication of the worst forms of child labor, including the recruitment and engagement of child soldiers, and, by 2025, fully eradicating child labor in all its forms.
- By 2020, considerably reducing the share of youth not engaged in employment, educational, or professional training.
- Protection of labor rights and assistance to create safe working conditions for all employees, including migrant employees, and in particular female migrant employees, and individuals employed in non-standard professions.
- By 2030, developing, and introducing a sustainable tourism policy that will create jobs and promote local culture and goods.
- Strengthen the potential of internal financial institutions to stimulate and widen access to banks, and insurance and financial services for everyone.
- Expansion of assistance for supporting trade with developing countries, in particular with the least developed countries, including via the advanced integrated framework program of technical assistance in trade to the least developed countries.

- By 2020, developing, and introducing the UN Global Jobs Compact by the International Labor Organization.

Taking into account this global trend and global goal integrates the Far Eastern region and all of Russia into a civilized world community with contemporary civilization employment relations.

4.1.3 Job Digitalization

According to forecasts of top expert agencies, in the close future over 47% of legal workplaces in the USA will be digitalized, i.e., computer software or robots will replace employees.[7] In the opinion of researchers, 54% of workplaces in the EU are at risk of computerization.[8]

In the opinion of a number of authors, in this case, the digitalizing of routine and physically burdensome professions will enable the improvement of labor productivity and adjust employment patterns toward the provision of various services.[9] Thus, digitalization reduces demand for the workforce and entails unemployment in some sectors, but accompanies the growth of employment in the manufacturing of new digital goods and services.[10]

Digitalizing results in cost-saving that will affect the lowering of prices for certain goods and services which, in turn, can release

7. Greene, L., & Mamic, I. *The Future of Work: Increasing Reach Through Mobile Technology*; Greene, L., & Mamic, I., (2015). *DWT for East and South-East Asia and the Pacific*. Bangkok: ILO. http://www.ilo.org/wcmsp5/groups/public/---asia/---ro-bangkok/---sro-bangkok/documents/publication/wcms_342162.pdf (accessed on 9 June 2020).
8. Berger, T., & Frey, C., (2016). *Structural Transformation in the OECD: Digitalization, Deindustrialization, and the Future of Work*. OECD Social, Employment, and Migration Working Papers, No. 193, OECD Publishing, Paris. http://dx.doi.org/10.1787/5jlr068802f7-en (accessed on 9 June 2020).
9. *Ibid.*
10. Spiezia, V., & Marco, V., (2016). What do we know about the effects of information and communication technologies on employment levels? In: Greenan, N., L'Horty, Y., & Mairesse, J., (eds.), *Productivity, Inequality, and the Digital Economy: A Transatlantic Perspective*. Cambridge: MIT Press.

resources for additional investment and consumption of other goods and services, and hence, contributes to the growth of employment in these sectors and fields.[11]

According to the McKinsey Global Institute's estimates,[12] information, and communications technologies can replace about 140 million of full-time white-collar workers all over the world.[12] However, referring to the Polanyi paradox[13] ("we know more than we can tell"), some researchers note that a wide range of jobs might not be automated, since they involve tasks that require intuition or judgment.[14] Thus, in the opinion of C. B. Frey and M. A. Osborn,[15] computer technologies are not yet capable of implementing the following characteristics of workplaces: social profile, creativity, the ability to take non-standard, novel solutions, and to manipulate, influence, and control a human. Moreover, according to C. B. Frey and T. Berger, "[there] is no evidence to suggest that the computer revolution so far has reduced overall demand for jobs as technologically stagnant sectors of the economy—including health care, government, and personal services—continue to create vast employment opportunities. Looking forward, however, we argue that as the potential scope of automation is expanding, many sectors that have been technologically stagnant in the past are likely to become technologically progressive in the future."[16]

11. OECD. *ICTS and Jobs: Complements or Substitutes? The Effects of ICT Investment on Labor Demand by Skill and by Industry in Selected OECD Countries*, forthcoming.
12. MGI, (2013). *Disruptive Technologies: Advances That Will Transform Life, Business, and the Global Economy.* Tech. Rep., McKinsey Global Institute. http://www.mckinsey.com/mgi/overview (accessed on 9 June 2020).
13. Polanyi, M., (1966). *The Tacit Dimension.* New York, Doubleday.
14. Autor, D. H., (2015). Why are there still so many jobs? The history and future of workplace automation. *The Journal of Economic Perspectives, 29*(3), 3–30.
15. Frey, C. B., & Osborne, M. A., (2013). *The Future of Employment: How Susceptible are Jobs to Computerization?* http://www.oxfordmartin.ox.ac.uk/downloads/academic/The_Future_of_Employment.pdf (accessed on 9 June 2020)
16. Berger, T., & Frey, C., (2016). *Structural Transformation in the OECD: Digitalization, Deindustrialization, and the Future of Work.* OECD Social, Employment, and Migration Working Papers, No. 193, OECD Publishing, Paris. http://dx.doi.org/10.1787/5jlr068802f7-en (accessed on 9 June 2020).

One must note that those occupations and workplaces would only become digitalized if the alternative cost of their digitalized equivalents is less than the workforce labor price.[17] Respectively, it does not pay to computerize and automate low-paid jobs. Therefore, they will be transferred to under-developed countries with low living standards or will attract migrant workers and local low-level workers.[18] Lack of government control over these economic activities and insufficient material support of low-paid resident groups will provoke the development of precarious employment among such population groups.

It is important to understand that jobs produce certain goods and services that are available for purchase and consumption. If a consumer is not prepared for their digital equivalents, a workplace cannot be digitalized. Respectively, digitalization is possible in the event of the relevant development of digital competences both in a producer and a consumer.

Here we can trace a new need, too, i.e., being capable to interact with artificial intelligence (AI), i.e., the creation of employees' digital competence and, as a consequence, the digital potential of employment. What should an employee be in this interactive process: the creator of an interaction who is subject to AI or who controls AI?

In our work, we substantiate the following economical categories necessary for analysis of this interaction:

An employee's digital competence (EDC) is a part of human potential shown in labor potential and implemented by using ICT. EDC is an employee's skills (created and changing) that enable the employee to function in the economy, and to use ICT in his/her activities.[19]

---

17. OECD Employment Outlook, (2017). http://dx.doi.org/10.1787/empl_outlook-2017-en (accessed on 9 June 2020).
18. Autor, D. H., & David, D., (2013). The growth of low-skill service jobs and the polarization of the U.S. Labor Market. *American Economic Review, 103*(5), 1533–1597.
19. Novikova, I. V., (2018). Classifications of information competence of an employee and information competences of workplaces. Forsyte Russia: New Industrial Society. Reset. In: Bodrunov, S. D., (ed.), *Book of reports of the St. Petersburg International Economic Congress (SPEC-2017)* (Vol. 2, pp. 669–679). St. Petersburg.

The digital potential of employment is a social and economic potential formed during the interaction of an employee's digital competence and the digital components of a workplace.[20]

Workplace digital components (WDCs) are social and economic indicators of constituent elements and requirements to the organization and functioning of a workplace that contribute to the implementation of an employee's digital competence.[21] The types of digital potential of employment are presented in Figure 4.2.

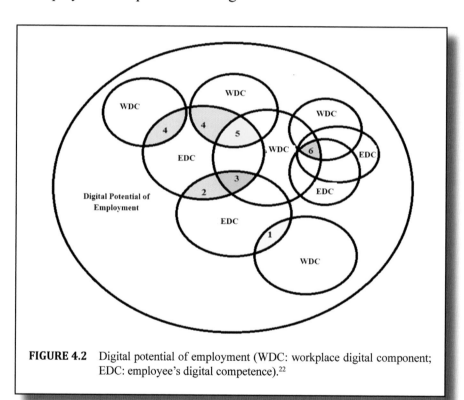

FIGURE 4.2 Digital potential of employment (WDC: workplace digital component; EDC: employee's digital competence).[22]

---

20. Novikova, I. V., (2017). *Regulation of Employment in the Russian Far East*. Moscow: RUSCIENCE.
21. *Ibid.*
22. *Ibid.*

- **Form 1 (Basic DPE):** Interaction between digital competence of an employee and digital components of a workplace;
- **Form 2:** Interaction between digital competence of one employee and digital competence of the other employee regardless of the digital components of a workplace;
- **Form 3:** Interaction between digital competence of two or several employees and digital components of one workplace;
- **Form 4:** Interaction between digital competence of an employee and different digital components of two (several) workplaces;
- **Form 5:** Interaction between digital competence of one employee with similar digital components of two (several) workplaces;
- **Form 6:** Simultaneous interaction between digital competences of two or several employees with digital components of two (several) workplaces.

Bilateral interaction forms are the basis for building more complex interaction forms. Interaction between an employee's digital competence and WDCs carries a multiplicative effect capable of developing an employee's digital competence and expanding WDCs. Production performance depends on the closeness and accuracy of such interaction.

The workplace digitalization trend can be viewed as a threat to the development of the FEFD's workforce in the event of an untimely distribution of advanced ICT. However, in view of isolation, low population density, a workforce shortage in some economic sectors and activities, use of digital technologies and digitalized workplaces will give rise to the more effective development of the whole region and labor resources, in particular.

4.1.4   Removal of Geographical and Time Boundaries for Distribution of Workplaces

The development of ICT and their reduction in price and availability contribute to workplace deployment anywhere in the world[23] where there are relevant labor resources and inexpensive methods to get them. It is sufficient if there is potential workforce availability, i.e., a working-age population having certain human capital that can be adapted to fulfill certain workplace functions, and loyal state policy toward labor resources, enabling their use.[24] According to Rorunka and Kubicek in 2017,[25] "Vertical disintegration which preserves major competences and outsources other activities resulted in flexible networked economy and appearance of the global value chain."[25] Thus, workforce donor regions and workforce receiving regions appear.[26] Virtual migration occurs,[27] i.e., geographically the workforce remains at the place of its residence, but transfers results of its labor outside.

There are various employment formation options depending on how much a market can be digitalized. Moreover, a list of suitable jobs is widened for employees thus decreasing their interest in precarious employment forms. However, an employer also gets wider opportunities for personnel selection and recruitment, including to precarious vacancies.

23. Eurofound and the International Labor Office, (2017). *Working Anytime, Anywhere: The Effects on the World of Work.* Publications Office of the European Union, Luxembourg, and the International Labor Office, Geneva.
24. Est, R. V., & Kool, L., (2015). *Working on the Robot Society: Visions and Insights from Science Concerning the Relationship Between Technology and Employment* (p. 55). The Hague, Rathenau Instituut.
25. Rorunka, C., & Kubicek, B., (2017). *Job Demands in a Changing World of Work: Impact on Workers' Health and Performance and Implication for Research and Practice.* Vienna, Austria.
26. Berger, T., & Frey, C., (2016). *Structural Transformation in the OECD: Digitalization, Deindustrialization, and the Future of Work.* OECD Social, Employment, and Migration Working Papers, No. 193, OECD Publishing, Paris. http://dx.doi.org/10.1787/5jlr068802f7-en (accessed on 10 June 2020).
27. Cristiano, C., Fabienne, A., & Federico, B. *The Future of Work in the "Sharing Economy": Market Efficiency and Equitable Opportunities or Unfair Precarisation?* Institute for Prospective Technological Studies, JRC Science for Policy Report, EUR 27913 EN. doi: 10.2791/431485.

For instance, if a job can be performed indirectly and does not requires face-to-face interaction,[28] or if tasks of that job can be digitalized,[29] a workplace can be outsourced offshore.

According to estimates of Van Welsum and Reif, 20% of the OECD's employment have the potential to be moved offshore.[30]

The Russian Far East borders with the most advanced powers in the development of informational and communication technologies. Consequently, there are opportunities for the active engagement of highly-skilled professionals, gaining experiences and developing the digital economy in the region, and the economy which will let residents of the Russian Far East perform work remotely, without having to migrate to more decent workplaces in other regions.

However, if this trend is ignored, it may result in a greater decline in the region due to the fact that high-income jobs become digitalized, or moved offshore, or get outsourced, while the local workforce will perform only low-income labor functions which, respectively, will impact their quality of life.

4.1.5 Generation of Millennials (Generation Y) Entering the Employment Market

Generation Y, a principally new workforce generation, is entering the employment market; for Generation Y digital technologies are a part of their ordinary life routine since childhood.[31] These young men and women are more adapted to digitalization, which provides them

28. Blinder, & Alan, S., (2016). Offshoring: the next industrial revolution? *Foreign Affairs*, *85.2*, p. 113.
29. Berger, T., & Frey, C., (2016). *Structural Transformation in the OECD: Digitalization, Deindustrialization, and the Future of Work*. OECD Social, Employment, and Migration Working Papers, No. 193, OECD Publishing, Paris http://dx.doi.org/10.1787/5jlr068802f7-en (accessed on 10 June 2020).
30. Van Welsum, D., & Reif, X., (2015). Potential offshoring: Evidence from selected OECD countries, *Brookings Trade Forum*, Brookings Institution Press, 165–194.
31. Novikova, I. V., (2016). Flexible employment as a form of materialization of an "info man's" ability to work. *Bulletin of Samara State University of Economics*, *2*(136), 70–76.

with certain competitive strengths against older adults. Their digital competences (skills) enable them to use practically all digitalization opportunities and minimize most of their threats; therefore, millennials may be called "info humans."

A so-called "info human"[32] has the digital competences of an employee, i.e., qualities (formed and changing) that enable him/her to function in the economy, and use informational and communications technologies in his/her activities.[33] Such qualities include new ways of thinking, flexible employment, continuous educational and professional development, mobility, and the free use of informational and communication technologies in all spheres of life.[34] The compliance of these employee competences with digital components will result in the growth of labor productivity, and decrease employment fluctuations.

An "info human" is also able to lower transaction costs of information searches (as to training, professional development, suitable jobs, "honest" employers), job placement (electronic CVs, online interviews with employers), and employment (remote employment, telework, etc.). Therefore, the growth in the number of individuals possessing properties of "info human" will contribute to the expansion of various employment forms that meet the needs of the economy and the able-bodied population.

An "info human" treasures his/her leisure time and seeks to form a balance between personal life and working time.[35] This feature may

32. Novikova, I. V., (2016). "Info man" is a basis of future labor resources. *Book of Article Abstracts from Readings at Mikhail Lomonosov* (pp. 58–59). International Scientific Conference. *Economics and Development of University-Based Schools of Thought* (on the occasion of the 75th anniversary of the Faculty of Economics at Lomonosov Moscow State University). Moscow: Faculty of Economics of Lomonosov Moscow State University.
33. Novikova, I. V., (2017). *Regulation of Employment in the Russian Far East.* Moscow: RUSCIENCE.
34. Employment, Skills, and Human Capital Global Challenge Insight Report, (2016). *The Future of Jobs Employment, Skills, and Workforce Strategy for the Fourth Industrial Revolution.* World Economic Forum. http://www3.weforum.org/docs/Media/WEF_Future-ofJobs.pdf (accessed on 10 June 2020).
35. Eurofound and the International Labor Office, (2017). *Working Anytime, Anywhere: The Effects on the World of Work.* Publications Office of the European Union, Luxembourg, and the International Labor Office, Geneva.

be used to develop the peripheral regions where a shortage of decent permanent jobs leads to emigration, depopulation of a territory, and other accompanying negative effects, including precarization. Getting opportunities for education, jobs, and remote employment contributes to workforce migration in digital forms without physical relocation. Respectively, income earned from teleworking will be spent in the local markets of goods and services, forming a multiplicative effect of employment growth at local labor markets with permanent workplaces.

The development of an info human's competences in the Russian Far East will enable the aggregation of frontline technologies and modern resources to the region, and will increase quality of life and living standards of the population.

4.1.6   Income Differentiation

Digitalization influences income redistribution of the population and business. There is an opportunity to use informational and communication technologies to improve labor productivity and profitability, including raising wages.

A weak point is insufficient or zero use of digital components of workplaces resulting in the loss of competition with more technologically equipped companies. The advantages of digitalization will be distributed everywhere, but only if the markets work well.

If the product market is small, productivity gain will not be able to lead to the reduction of prices, and the growing demand for jobs. If nominal wages are not flexible, some employees might get higher real wages, while others will become unemployed. Thus, without the proper regulation of the labor market and an effective competition policy, digital technologies may finally have greater distribution effects and increase the income gap between various population groups.[36]

---

36.   New Market and New Jobs of the OECD Ministerial Meeting on the Digital Economy, (2016). Cancún (Mexico). *OECD Digital Economy Papers, No. 255.*

The growth in differentiation of the population income in the Russian Far East as compared to other regions is the main reason for workforce outflow from the FEFD. The positive Soviet-era experience of Far Eastern compensations and guarantees may be used in the present provided that it is radically adjusted to market conditions. The author's approaches to the application of the Far Eastern guarantees are given above in this book.

4.1.7 Non-Standard Employment Forms

In contemporary conditions, new employment forms are developing:

- **Strategic Employee Sharing:** A group of employers sets up a network that hires one or several employees to deliver performance individual jobs together with participating corporate employers;
- **Job Sharing:** An employer hires two or more employees for the joint fulfillment of work;
- **Interim Management:** A company hires another company's employee to fulfill a temporary job or a certain work task;
- **Casual Work:** Employment is not stable and permanent, and an employer is not obliged to provide work to its employee but can act flexibly and call an employee for work at short notice;
- **Intermittent Work:** An employer periodically (or from time-to-time) recruits employees to fulfill a certain job often related to an individual project or for a seasonal job. Employment is characterized by a fixed deadline, including task performance, or a certain number of working days;
- **On-Call Work (Zero-Hours Contracts):** Permanent/continuous employment relationship maintained between an employer and an employee, but an employer does not provide permanent work for its employee but, rather, an employer may call an employee as necessary;

- **Full Mobility:** Frequent changes of job locations and multiple job locations with various job change models and combination of individual and collective workplaces;
- **Site Mobility:** Mobility within a job site with frequent location changes but within geographically limited areas;
- **Multi-Location Workplaces:** Several fixed workplaces to be changed not often, but with special mobility;
- **Networked Workplaces:** Limited physical mobility, but with work possible in various locations; jobs thus fulfilled involve twenty-four-hour development of software and complicated engineering and technical tasks;
- **Voucher-Based Work:** An employer buys a voucher from a third party (generally a governmental authority), which will be used as payment for a service provided by an employee, and not by cash;
- **Portfolio Workers:** Employees have several workplaces or several contracts in various fields and with various companies;
- **Ad Hoc Employee Sharing:** An employee, which for the time being cannot provide work to its employees, sends them to do work at another company (the employment contract between an original employer and the employee remains effective as long as the employee is enlisted into the personnel of the recipient employer);
- **Crowd Employment:** Using an online platform which enables organizations or individuals to get access to an indefinite or an unknown group of other organizations or private persons to solve specific problems or provide specific services or goods in return for payment;
- **Collaborative Employment:** Cooperation between part-time employees, individual entrepreneurs, and micro-enterprises for the provision of specific services or the performance of specific work;

- **Umbrella Organizations:** Provision of specific administrative services such as billing clients or the settlement of tax issues.[37]

The advantages of non-standard employment forms consist in the ability to flexibly combine work and private life, work duration, and schedule, building value chains.[38] Using these diverse employment forms will enable the improvement of efficiency in the Russian Far East's businesses and integrate the region into the global employment market.

4.1.8 Online Platforms

Online platforms where an employee and the customer of the employee's work directly interact get widespread use in digitalization conditions as a new form of employment. They contain potential numerous opportunities and threats. A study conducted by McKinsey Global Institute showed that online platforms may ensure GDP growth at the global level of USD 2.7 trillion benefiting 540 million persons by means of increasing participation in the employment market and labor productivity.[39]

Some platforms such as TaskRabbit, Handy, or Youpijob, provide a market for low-skilled workers with casual earnings. Other platforms

37. Eurofound and the International Labor Office, (2017). *Working Anytime, Anywhere: The effects on the World of Work.* Publications Office of the European Union, Luxembourg, and the International Labor Office, Geneva. http://www.trudcontrol.ru/files/editor/files/wcms_544138.pdf (accessed on 10 June 2020).
38. Greene, L., & Mamic, I., (2015). *The Future of Work: Increasing Reach through Mobile Technology;* Greene, L., & Mamic, I., (2016). *ILO DWT for East and South-East Asia and the Pacific.* Bangkok: ILO, Panel 4.2 "Skills for a Digital World" of the OECD Ministerial Meeting on the Digital Economy, Cancún (Mexico). http://www.oecd-ilibrary.org/docserver/download/5jlwz83z3wnw-en.pdf?expires=1492081762&id=id&accname=guest&checksum=D83D1D2946C28760EC4645B3337E320B (accessed on 10 June 2020); Eurofound and the International Labor Office, (2017). *Working Anytime, Anywhere: The Effects on the World of Work.* Publications Office of the European Union, Luxembourg, and the International Labor Office, Geneva. http://www.trudcontrol.ru/files/editor/files/wcms_544138.pdf (accessed on 10 June 2020).
39. McKinsey Global Institute, (2015). *A Labor Market that Works: Connecting Talent with Opportunity in the Digital Age: Highlights.* Washington: McKinsey & Company.

such as Upwork, Freelancer, or Nubelo provide digital services online, balance supply and demand in various countries, perform a wide range of tasks from low-skilled ones, such as data input, to administrative support by highly-skilled professions, e.g., programming, or legal or business consulting.

The platforms allow considerable change to conventional work mechanisms and relationships in the employment market. Some full-time permanent workplaces transform into a pulsating flow ("on-demand") of tasks for a large global pool of "virtual workers." Although these changes create opportunities for employees, job seekers, and companies, they also create serious problems for work quality, taxation, and social welfare.[40]

The platforms contributed to the creation of workplaces during the economic crisis and can create additional employment opportunities in the Far Eastern Region while mitigating the shortage of skills in dynamic fields. Moreover, since workplaces require small investments and training from employers, they seem suitable for small and medium enterprises (SME), as well as local authorities and social responsible businesses. At that, increased outsourcing of tasks to other regions and countries may result in loss of workplaces in the local and national employment markets.[41]

The concept of the FEFD's Workforce Development Strategy is based on proposals by the Global Commission on the Future of Work,[42] set up in 2017 by the International Labor Organization. The basic postulate approved by this Commission was the decision that a human is the core element in the economy.

---

40. New Market and New Jobs of the OECD Ministerial Meeting on the Digital Economy, (2016). Cancún (Mexico). *OECD Digital Economy Papers, No. 255.*
41. *Eurofound New Forms of Employment* (2015). Publications Office of the European Union, Luxembourg. doi.org/10.2806/989252.
42. Working for the Better Future (2019). *Global Commission on the Future of Work, International Labor Office* (p. 21). Geneva: MBT.

The initiative stipulates the necessity of:

1. An increase of investments in the development of human capabilities (implementation of the general right for life-long education, which allows people to acquire professional skills, retrain, and advance in skill); an increase of investments in institutions, policy, and strategies that will support people in the course of transitional processes in future work fields (youth, elderly employees, women returning to work after a childcare leave, etc., ensuring of general social welfare from birth to old age; and a gender equality guarantee);

2. An increase of investments into employment market institutes (setting a universal labor guarantee, such as decent wages, setting maximum duration of working hours, occupational safety and health; enhancing independent time control; ensuring collective representation of employees and employers with active government assistance; and introducing and using technologies in the interests of decent work);

3. An increase of investments in decent and secure employment (the creation of stimuli for investments in key fields for decent and secure employment; adjustment of the business incentive structure in the interests of investment approaches and the creation of additional indicators of human development and welfare).

The concept of the FEFD's Workforce Development Strategy is based on the following statutory and regulatory enactments that reflect national trends:

1. The concept of long-term social and economic development of the Russian Federation for the period until 2020 to implement the target reference point "Economy of Leadership and Innovations," which involves the arrangement of conditions for the

mass emergence of new innovative companies in all economy sectors and, as a priority, in the knowledge economy.

2. The Strategy of Development for an Information Society for the years 2017–2030 in terms of implementing the strategic priorities:

- Developing the information and communication infrastructure of the Russian Federation;
- Creating and using Russian ICT, ensuring their competitiveness at the international level;
- Forming a new technological basis to develop the economic and social sphere.

3. The program "Digital Economy of the Russian Federation" within the framework of implementing the goals related to information infrastructure:

- Developing communication networks that provide for the needs of the economy related to the collection of governmental, business, and personal data with an allowance for requirements provided by digital technologies;
- Developing a system of Russian data processing centers that ensures the provision to the State, businesses, and citizens of available, stable, secure, and economically efficient data storage and processing services on certain conditions and allows, among other things, exporting data storage and processing services;
- Introducing digital data handling platforms to meet the needs of the State, businesses, and individuals;
- Establishing an efficient spatial data collection, processing, storage, and client provision system that meets the needs of the State, businesses, and citizens for actual and reliable information about spatial objects.

Regional trends were determined in the Russian Federation State Program "Social and Economic Development of the Russian Far East and Baikal Region" and "Action Plan for Personnel Training in Key Sectors of the Economy of the Far Eastern Federal District (FEFD) and Support of Youth in the Employment Market Through 2025."

The said enactments reflect the resource orientation of the territory's development and the respective need in workforce training and employment.

4.2 WORKFORCE DEVELOPMENT: MISSION AND VISION

The FEFD has great environmental assets. The FEFD is a Russian region of geostrategic importance and is characteristic of very low density and labor deficits.

1. **Mission:** The creation in the region of required conditions for achieving high working life quality standards conforming to the standards of developed countries in the Asia Pacific region, on the basis of using cutting-edge developments in ICT and new effective employment forms, and the principles of a green economy and decent "green" workplaces.
2. **Vision:** The territory and available competitive strengths of the FEFD allow the creation of comfort conditions to implement the potential of a decent population employment system. Advanced use of cutting-edge equipment and technologies, and the creation of a green economy and decent green jobs will create in this territory a region with whole new and improved living conditions for the population; this will make the region attractive both within the country and abroad.

The Implementation of the Strategy will allow the forming of following competitive strengths of a Far Eastern employee.

A Far Easterner is someone who:

- Possesses knowledge and skills of communication and interaction with nationals of APR countries;
- Is highly tolerant to people of different confessions, ethnic groups, and cultures;
- Is capable of life-long development, self-improvement, and education;
- Has digital competences and is capable of training, working, receiving, and providing services by means of ICT;
- Identifies with all nationals of the Russian Federation;
- Is highly cultured with a cultural background that is a fusion of multinational cultures of the Far Eastern Region, including loyalty to foreign cultures of APR countries;
- Takes good care of the environment and can operate within a green economy;
- Can, on his or her own, set and solve numerous objectives without external assistance;
- Binds his/her decent life and life of his/her children and grand-children with the FEFD.

The principles of workforce development are:

- The necessity to provide conditions for advanced development of the FEFD in all national programs, and legal and regulatory enactments to be developed and adopted;
- The development of a balanced model of employment regulation in the region and relevant model implementation strategy on the basis of creating and maintaining conditions for the effective and decent employment of the population;
- The development of a full-scale regional information-communication space compliant with global-level ICT, full-

scale inclusion into an all-Russian and global information and communication space in view of implementing these distance employment forms;

- The arrangement of an effective system for providing governmental Far Eastern guarantees for employed residents of the region aimed at improving the region's attraction for permanent residents and new settlers;
- Ensuring that ecological cleanness is maintained in the region by creating and developing a green economy and green workplaces as well.

4.3 OTSW ANALYSIS OF WORKFORCE DEVELOPMENT IN THE FAR EASTERN FEDERAL DISTRICT (FEFD)

Opportunities	Threats
Establishment of new innovative enterprises based on use of information and communication technologies; setting up green companies that among other things use recycling opportunities; arrangement of high-quality conditions for employee's digital competences; lowering production costs by reducing labor charges, active introduction of distance employment, e-trading, and electronic payments into manufacturing and sales processes; reduction of clandestine employment in the shadow economy by getting employees interested in receiving clean official wages; development of a public-private partnership in employment system; minimizing of territorial and sectoral disbalance between labor supply and demand by spreading distance employment forms; improvement of control effectiveness and supervision of compliance with labor laws and other statutory and regulatory enactments that contain employment and labor statutes, and compliance by parties to the social partnership with contracts and collective agreements.	Conditions being in place for undermining of integrity of the country territory; environmental degradation; reduction of the able-bodied population, and migration of the able-bodied population to central regions of Russia and abroad; displacement of personnel and job cuts as a result of technology modernization in various economy sectors plus massive engagement of the migrant workforce; reducing opportunities for the employment of individual population groups who are not competitive in the labor market; negative changes in the political and economic situation in the country; changes in the interests of foreign partners to the region; changes in central authorities' attitude towards the region's development trends; China's strategic interests as to the transfer of environmentally-dangerous production facilities.

Strengths	Weaknesses
Large territory of the region (33% of the total area of the Russian Federation); profitable geo-economic position of the Region in proximity to rapidly developing APR countries; rich natural resources potential; great natural and climatic diversity; sufficiently environmentally-clean territory; developed research and educational complex with all professional training and general education levels; developed healthcare system; availability of special governmental programs and legal enactments aimed at supporting and developing the region; implementation of special governmental support of SM businesses in the region; well-run system of regulating the influx of foreign workers; interest of federal and regional authorities in developing this region; availability in the region of a basis for sufficiently wide dissemination of information and communication technologies; Prevalence (among residents of the region) of working-aged and younger individuals capable of training and retraining.	Lack of a permanent and common vision by the State as to the development of this region and the reasonableness of a certain number of the population residing in the region; no region development program and strategy are completely fulfilled; low population density; low motivation of the population for living in the FEFD; insufficient number of highly skilled professionals in the region's economy; lack of a single coordinator of business and educational institutions' interaction in education and retraining of sought-after specialists; there is a territorial and structural disbalance in labor supply and demand in the employment markets; high-level shadow economy and unreported employment; considerable inter-regional differences by economic activity and living standards; negative population growth in the region not balanced with external migration; low workforce mobility within the region; misbalance between salary level and labor productivity resulting in lowering motivation of employees; insufficient development of cooperation ties between educational institutions and businesses; insufficient development of parties in public-private partnership that represent the interests of employees and employers; high share of residents insufficiently competitive in the labor market; Low competitiveness of goods and services produced in the region because of high labor charges.

4.4 COMPETITIVE STRENGTHS IN WORKFORCE DEVELOPMENT

The main competitive strength of workforce development in the FEFD is the official concern of the Russian State in use of this territory and resources. In light of this fact, numerous regulatory documents, programs, decrees, and statutory enactments are developed, special-purpose governmental agencies are established (such as the "Far Eastern hectare," "advanced development territories (ADTs)," etc.) aimed at developing the labor resources of the Russian Far East.

Moreover, vocational education and training systems are already established in the region (61 professional educational institutions that train skilled worker and, office employees are included in Far Eastern Federal University[43]), and, in accordance with the Directive of the RF government dated August 18, 2018,[44] the system will be expanded, although insignificantly, and only within the needs of the region as envisaged by the governmental authorities.

A considerable competitive strength for the labor resources of the Russian Far East is the geographical proximity to, and well-established partnership relations with, advanced economies of Japan, China, Korea, and the USA. These are rapidly developing countries whose educational and professional potential can be effectively used for the development of local labor resources.

One of the major competitive strengths of the FEFD is a vast territory that is environmentally clean and in some areas quite wild. In a situation with growing environmental hazards, this competitive strength provides great opportunities for the region. These are areas attractive for living in an environmentally clean place, developing environmentally clean agriculture, and manufacturing organic products, i.e., the development of a green economy and green jobs that are sought-after all over the world.

1. **Workforce Development Goal:** Establishing in the region of employment a system capable of ensuring the development of a competitive economy based on the use of various employment forms, decent, and green workplaces, and the wide use of ICT.

2. **Workforce Development Objectives:**

    i. Conducting an educational policy aimed at improving the quality of labor resources and their conformity to employers' needs;

---

43. Regions of Russia, (2017). *Socio-Economic Indicators*. www.gks.ru (accessed on 10 June 2020).

44. Executive Order of the RF Government, (2018). No. 1727, "Program of actions in training of personnel for key sectors of the economy of the Far Eastern Federal District and youth support in the labor market through to 2025."

ii. Increasing the attractiveness of the region for residence and employment;

iii. Developing an institutional employment regulation environment including public-private partnership institutes;

iv. Developing decent green jobs and a green economy;

v. setting up high-quality labor potential that will become a calling card of Russian labor resources for APR countries.

4.5 STRATEGIC PRIORITIES IN WORKFORCE DEVELOPMENT

The setting up and expansion of businesses based on the active use of ICT in the region.

1. Main Activities:

- Training personnel who are able to function at modern enterprises using ICT;
- Taking measures to improve labor productiveness by means of the efficient use of an employee's digital competence;
- Developing the information and communication technology sector, which will provide cutting-edge equipment and technologies;
- Developing public-private partnerships in the introduction and use of ICT;
- Actively developing e-businesses;
- Forming and disseminating a self-employment system by using ICT;
- Developing ICT-based distance employment forms;
- Setting up ICT-based technology parks;
- Developing e-commerce;
- Improving the taxation of e-businesses, distance employment, and e-commerce;

- Establishing the Far Eastern Department of Distance Development of the Region.

The prototypes for the Far Eastern Department of Distance Development of the Region are digital technology centers established in developed countries.[45] The Far Eastern Department will include the following activities:

- **Analytical Activities:**
  - Monitoring distance workplaces in the region and beyond the region, including abroad;
  - Monitoring vacant distance workplaces in the region and beyond the region, including abroad;
  - Monitoring distance educational programs of various levels and directions of training, retraining, and advanced training;
  - Monitoring distance self-employment forms in Russia and abroad.

- **Prognostic Activities:**
  - Participation in developing economic development forecasts for the region with an account of distance activities (employment and training);
  - Participation in developing the region's social development forecasts with an account of distance activities (employment and training).

---

45. Adam, D., Campbell-Hall, V., De Hoyos, M., Green, A., & Thomas, A., (2011). Increasing digital channel use amongst Jobcentre Plus claimants. *DWP Research Report*. http://research.dwp.gov.uk/asd/asd5/rports2011-2012/rrep776.pdf (accessed on 10 June 2020); BIS National Plan for Digital Participation, (2010). *Department for Business Innovation and Skills*. http://raceonline2012.org/sites/default/files/resources/national-plan-digital-participation-final.pdf (accessed on 10 June 2020).

- **Introduction Activities:**
  - Introducing Internet communication at all levels and lines of development in the region;
  - Propagating distance activity forms among the population, using all Web platforms and mass media, and holding mass events for the popularization of these activity and educational forms;
  - Developing educational products required by the market using contemporary interactive training methods;
  - Training schoolchildren under distance education programs according to the school curriculum and in an in-depth form;
  - Training workers under distance education programs in the framework of elementary education;
  - Training semi-skilled workers under distance education programs;
  - Training highly-skilled workers under distance education programs;
  - Retraining employees of all levels using distance training programs;
  - Advanced training of employees of all levels using distance training programs;
  - Training in distance job placement and activities;
  - Providing consulting and legal support to residents who train and conduct activities in the distance form;
  - Providing consulting support in the establishment and conducting of distance businesses;
  - Establishing co-working stations in cities and district centers that are suited for distance learning or distance activities. These co-working stations will simultaneously provide conditions for activities (computer, internet access, desk, chair, and meeting room) and will include an advisor on distance activities who will answer any arising questions.

Conducting a social policy aimed at improving the regional population's quality of working life of the population on the basis of ICT technologies.

2. **Core Activities:**

- **Education:**
    - Improving the population's digital literacy to create necessary consumers, sellers, producers, and employees;
    - Introducing into all educational programs of all levels the elements aimed at Teaching the population how to act in a digital society;
    - Creating an ICT-based mechanism of evaluation for educational programs;
    - Establishing educational institutions of all levels that conduct their activities only on the basis of distance learning, and introducing ICT technologies into the work of stationary educational institutions for conducting educational processes with remote users;
    - Introducing ICT technologies into the work of educational institutions at all levels for access to databases in the country and abroad;
    - Continuous advanced training of teachers for work in a digital society; for being able to use contemporary ICT technologies and apply them in educational processes; to have competences for training a modern person;
    - The creation and functioning of universal and specialized portals containing comprehensive data about educational processes and systems, including structure, elements, mobility, etc.:
    - Developing and continuous updating of educational content based on the latest global digital resources;

- o The creation and functioning of network universities, institutes, and other institutions of vocational training and retraining;
- o Creating an ICT-based mechanism for occupational guidance, and building up career strategies;
- o Creating an ICT-based mechanism for identifying new and future sought-after occupations in a digital society;
- o Creating a promptly updated ICT-based database for these knowledges, skills, and employee competences;
- o Creating an effective system of distance and stationary training aimed at expanding employment capabilities for the elderly generation, including distance employment forms;
- o Establishing an ICT-based proactive education system using ICT options;
- o Developing a system of compensating education costs in the event of consequent employment in the FEFD within at least five years.

- **Healthcare:**
  - o Actively introducing distance technologies into healthcare centers, enabling world-class medical treatment, diagnostics, medical consulting, and preventive treatment;
  - o Introducing multi-functional mobile stations into healthcare centers' operations, which would be equipped with modern equipment capable of autonomous distance interaction with leading medical centers;
  - o Guaranteed financing of professional consultations in specialist physicians' medical services for FEFD residents, including coverage of transport costs and accommodation charges for patients and their attendants;
  - o Compensating costs forgetting professional medical education in the leading medical institutions in Russia and abroad providing subsequent employment in the FEFD's territory.

- **Culture and Sport:**
  - ○ Providing full financing by the State for cultural and sports organizations;
  - ○ Ensuring distance access to major cultural and sports events held in Russia and abroad;
  - ○ Providing full financing of trained teams or individuals at cultural and sports competitions of all levels;
  - ○ Organizing and conducting national and international mass cultural and sports events in the region;
  - ○ Providing full access to cultural and sports facilities for all concerned individuals including those with financial constraints;
  - ○ Opening branch offices of all modern cultural and sports facilities in the region.

- **Housing:**
  - ○ Developing special terms of mortgage credits for residents of the FEFD and individuals intending to resettle in the FEFD;
  - ○ Organizing public economy-class residential construction under hire purchase agreements;
  - ○ Subsidizing programs of construction for social infra-structure facilities and residential houses by Far Eastern enterprises and organizations for their personnel.

3. Organizing Decent Green Workplaces:

- **Agriculture:**
  - ○ Conducting a policy of a careful attitude to resources and stimulating the organization of agricultural production with low carbon emissions;
  - ○ Supporting small-scale producers transitioning to more productive and sustainable farming methods on the basis of developing technical and business skills, favorable social

welfare target investments into infrastructure, organizational structure, and co-financing.

- **Forestry:**
  - o Reducing forest devastation, restoring deteriorated forests, and extending sustainable forest management practices by providing support to stable forestry enterprises with highly-skilled personnel and good working conditions;
  - o Developing production and sales systems and payments for ecosystem services to the local population.

- **Fishing Industry:**
  - o Reducing overfishing;
  - o Restoring depleted fishery resources and stimulating stable capture levels by income compensation during unemployment periods;
  - o Ensuring access to training in occupations not related with fishery;
  - o Supporting alternative income-achieving opportunities.

- **Power Engineering:**
  - o Increasing energy consumption efficiency by regulation, transmitting price signals, and providing access to funding in combination with advanced training and widening of cooperation between administration and employees;
  - o Widening use of renewable energy sources;
  - o Providing access to modern energy sources for those who have no such access yet.

- **Resource-Intensive Sectors:**
  - o Assisting the ecologization of these sectors by the considerable decrease of pollution levels, energy consumption, and use of resources by regulation and stimuli combined with information dissemination, providing access to funding,

and developing the interaction between administration and employees both at economy sector and enterprise levels.

- **Waste Disposal and Recycling:**
  - ○ Mitigating waste-related risks and an increase in the level of recovering valuable materials from waste by increasing recycling volumes, upgrading the waste management sector by improving waste-recycling plant organization, instituting service contracts, and developing technical and entrepreneurial competences.

- **Buildings and Structures:**
  - ○ Implementing a maximum energy performance potential by adopting stringent standards for new construction projects;
  - ○ Stimulating the renovation of existing construction infrastructure on the basis of regulation, information distribution, governmental investments, and providing access to inexpensive funding for clients as well as opportunities in advanced training, professional certification, and improvement of working conditions in the construction industry.

- **Transport:**
  - ○ Transitioning to the use of energy-efficient vehicles and types of transport, in particular public transport, by means of fiscal policy, regulation, and the stimulation of consumers in combination with the development of technologies, advanced training, and the allocation of state investments into infrastructure.

4.6 MECHANISMS TO IMPLEMENT THE WORKFORCE DEVELOPMENT STRATEGY

A *regulatory mechanism* is aimed at developing the necessary legislative framework for implementing strategy. The main requirement for developed and adopted documents is their alignment. A fear of duplicating certain actions results in the fact that the adopted documents cannot function together. Certain necessary actions might be omitted, which hampers or makes the functioning of a certain system as a whole impossible. Any newly adopted document most commonly results in canceling the previous document and this may break the required chain of interactions.

The basis for a financial and budgetary mechanism to implement strategy should consist of regional, federal, and local programs. Implementation of the strategy involves coordinated activities for implementing projects and measures contemplated under the programs to be used in the FEFD with an allowance of funds in the governmental budget at all levels, including internal and external private investors.

An *institutional mechanism* involves setting up a system of coordinated infrastructure elements that contribute to the implementation of the strategy. This infrastructure includes the following three elements:

- Entities within the analytical unit, whose activities involves performance of a wide list of analytical works;
- Entities within the forecasting unit, whose activities are associated with the development of short-term, medium-term, and long-term economic development and employment forecasts with due allowance for developing ICT technologies and contemporary employment forms; and
- Entities within an introduction unit, whose activities are focused on implementing all measures developed by entities of the above units.

The core issue here is the use of Internet communications. All measures taken are to be made available to the general public—not only within the region and the country, but abroad.

An *organizational mechanism* includes a system for managing the strategy. The FEFD's executive authority in charge of implementing the strategy as a whole is the Russian Federation Ministry for Development of the Russian Far East. The main parties responsible for implementation of the Strategy are specified in Table 4.1.

TABLE 4.1 Parties Engaged in the Strategy's Implementation

Government Authorities	Other Responsible Parties
RF Government	R&D institutes
RF Ministry for the Development of the Russian Far East	Advanced development territories
Regional governments	Top employers
Administrations of region's constituents	Trade unions
Human Capital Development Agency in the Russian Far East	Educational institutions
Far East Development Corporation	Healthcare institutions
Far Eastern Department for Distance Development of the Region	Employment agencies

The responsible parties ensure:

1. **The Monitoring of:**
   - Distance workplaces in the region and beyond, including abroad;
   - Vacant distance workplaces in the region and beyond, including abroad;
   - Distance education programs of all levels and sectors of training, retraining, and advanced training;
   - Distance self-employment in Russian and abroad;
   - Labor markets in the region;
   - Unemployed citizens;
   - Vacant workplaces reported to employment agencies;
   - Insecure employers;
   - Social sectors of the region (including education and healthcare);
   - Unemployed citizens who are insecure employees;
   - Employers' structure and standing in the region;

- Demand for employees in the ADTs, and in other employers with business seats outside ADTs, including foreign employers (in the USA, China, Korea, Japan, etc.).

2. **The Development of:**

   - Forecasts of the region's economic and social development with due allowance for distance activity forms (employment and training);
   - Forecasts of the demand for employees, including distance employees;
   - Educational programs of institutions that provide various personnel training and retraining levels;
   - Forecasts of the region's economic and social development.

3. **The Provision of:**

   - Educational products required by the labor market using modern interactive learning methods;
   - Services in cities and district centers through co-working stations suited for conducting distance training or distance work activities;
   - High-quality products made available on preferential terms to residents of the FEFD;
   - Green production that will not deteriorate the quality of life of the region's population;
   - Distance workplaces;
   - World-class social infrastructure for enterprise employees;
   - The region's positive image.

4. **The Training of:**

   - Schoolchildren within distance education programs under school curriculums and in an in-depth format;
   - Workers under distance training programs within the skilled worker education system;
   - Employees of any skill level under distance training programs;

- (Retraining of) employees of any skill level under distance training programs;
- (Advanced training of) employees of any skill level under distance training programs;
- Workers for job placement and employment in distance format;

5. The Organization of:

- Consulting and legal assistance for citizens in distance training and distance activities;
- Consulting on the issues of establishment and doing distance business;
- Introducing Internet communications at all levels and lines of development in the region;
- Popularizing distance activity forms among the population by use of any Web platforms, mass media, and holding mass events aimed at the popularization of distance education and activity forms;
- Promoting distance employment with the participation of employers from other regions and countries;
- Holding occupational guidance events;
- Holding events aimed at improving positive image of the FEFD;
- Selecting priority investment projects suggested for implementation in the FEFD, and agreement of their interests with the population's interests, including in terms of employment opportunities and improvement of living standards in the region;
- Making the FEFD's living standards closer to average Russian indicators, and exceeding them in the future;
- Collaborating with schools and other educational institutions to establish and develop a continuous comprehensive education;
- Popularizing working occupations;

- Registration of the unemployed;
- Material support by the payment of unemployment benefits;
- Accumulating employers' claimed demands for employees and respectively informing other responsible parties in the strategy;
- Providing professional training places for students of various educational institutions;
- Informing all of the strategy's responsible parties about the opening and supposed opening of new vacancies so that they could be filled timely and promptly by trained personnel;
- Timely informing all of the strategy's responsible parties about reductions or forecast reductions in personnel in order to timely and promptly relocate employees to other vacancies;
- Using contemporary personnel management technologies and high-efficient ergonomic workplaces.

The diagram of interaction among infrastructure elements in this model is provided on Figure 4.3.

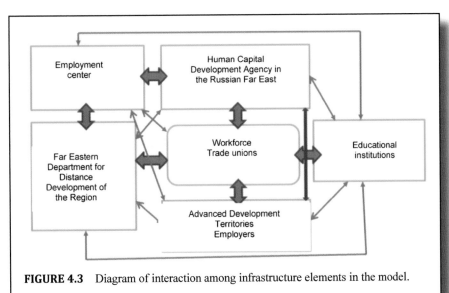

FIGURE 4.3   Diagram of interaction among infrastructure elements in the model.

Element interaction stages:

1. Labor Deficit Situation:

- The Human Capital Development Agency (HCDA) in the Russian Far East evaluates employment structure and dynamics.
- The Agency evaluates demands for employees of various levels and occupations.
- The Agency evaluates the balance between the needs of employers and the employed.
- Information is sent to the Far Eastern Department for Distance Development in the Region and to educational institutions.
- If the balance is positive (labor deficit), the responsible parties analyze the education system and begin to provide deficient labor resources. If required, curriculums, and training plans are to be adjusted according to the needs of employers.
- The Agency accesses information databases, including the All-Russian Vacancies Database "Jobs in Russia." It then requests information from ADTs and other employers about surplus labor resources for their redistribution to labor deficit economic sectors.
- If required, the Agency helps to transfer vacant workplaces to the distance mode and find an employee on distance employment terms.
- Internet communications are actively used in order to popularize vacant workplaces, sought-after occupations, employment forms, and territories with available workforce demand.

2. Labor Surplus Situation:

- The HCDA in the Russian Far East evaluates employment structure and dynamics.
- The Agency evaluates demand for employees of various levels and occupations.

- The Agency evaluates the balance between the needs of employers and the employed.
- Information is sent to the Far Eastern Department for Distance Development in the Region and to educational institutions.
- The Agency, acting jointly with Far Eastern Department for Distance Development in the Region and educational institutions, promptly adjusts educational programs by transferring to students to sought-after divisions.
- ADTs and employers, acting jointly with Far Eastern Department for Distance Development in the Region and educational institutions, begin proactive retraining of their employees who are potentially subject to personnel reduction plans. Proactive retraining was initiated in 1996 according to the Official Letter of the RF Federal Employment Service, dated August 12, 1996, and titled "On Proactive Vocational Training of Released Personnel." The proposed model involves distance retraining, thus minimizing corporate costs, including because of an employee's absence from his or her workplace during training.
- The Far Eastern Department for Distance Development in the Region actively performs training in distance work activities intending to support distance self-employment jobs.
- An employment center promptly registers applicants and transfers them to declared vacancies. If required, the center provides material support in the form of unemployment payments.
- The Far Eastern Department for Distance Development in the Region promotes the selection and recruitment of employees in other regions and countries on distance employment terms.
- The parties responsible actively use Internet communications aiming to popularize new and sought-after occupations, employment forms, and territories with workforce demand.

3. Balanced Employment Situation:

- The HCDA in the Russian Far East evaluates employment structure and dynamics.
- The Agency evaluates demand for employees of various levels and occupations.
- The Agency evaluates the balance between the needs of employers and the employed.
- Information is sent to the Far Eastern Department for Distance Development of the Region and to educational institutions.
- The Agency, acting jointly with Far Eastern Department for Distance Development in the Region and educational institutions, gradually adjusts educational programs in view of prospective changes to the economic situation and the needs of society and employees.
- The Far Eastern Department for Distance Development in the Region conducts training in sought-after fields taking into account both needs of employees for labor resources and needs of the whole society in getting various knowledge and skills.
- An employment center registers applicants and transfers them to declared vacancies. If required, the center provides material support in the form of unemployment payments.
- The Far Eastern Department for Distance Development in the Region promotes selection and recruitment of employees in other regions and countries on distance employment terms or employees from other regions at local distance workplaces.

4.7 SOCIAL AND ECONOMIC EFFECTS OF IMPLEMENTING THE STRATEGIC PRIORITIES

The social effect of implementing this strategy will consist in improving living standards in the Russian Far East and easing social tension in the region. The optimization of the personnel training process will lead to a reduction in unemployment at the cost of minimizing the dismissals of non-demanded employees who were forced out of their workplaces due to digitalization and were promptly retrained and moved to other workplaces.

A transparent policy of gradually implementing the workforce development strategy will contribute to a better image of the Russian Far East as a socially responsible employer and a territory of decent employment and living.

Green jobs will be the basis for developing a green economy in the region, which will help to preserve the environmentally clean situation in the Russian Far East which, in turn, will make this territory more attractive for living and working.

The distribution of ICT technologies and the development of digital competences will allow improved quality of life and living standards by increasing the availability of goods and services from all over the world. Residents of the Russian Far East will be able to receive world-class educational and medical services, and use virtual migration for their employment. This will result in the attraction of a highly-skilled workforce for permanent residence to the FEFD as a territory of comfortable living.

The economic effect from implementing the strategy will consist of:

- Reduction of costs for the dismissal, search, and recruitment of employees, including shutdown losses because of absence of required employees;
- Labor resources having better intrinsic motivation, since they understand their career strategy with possible transfer to other positions at enterprises in the region;
- Reduction in corporate expenses for personnel adaptation, teaching, training, and retraining;
- Increase in labor productivity and return on human capital.

KEYWORDS

- ➢ **artificial intelligence**
- ➢ **employee's digital competence**
- ➢ **Far Eastern Federal District**
- ➢ **global economic linkages**
- ➢ **International Institute for Labor Studies**
- ➢ **workplace digital components**
- ➢ **digital potential of employment**

Conclusion

The uniqueness of the Russian Far East in terms of its geographic position and natural resources, combined with the mentality of its residents tempered by the harsh conditions inherent in the area, bespeaks its great potential. To implement the region's competitive strengths, key elements of the concept "The FEFD's Workforce Development Strategy" were developed.

The implementation of digital technologies in all key areas of life allows taking down the barriers hindering proper development in the region. One of these barriers is the region's geographical and time-based isolation from the central regions of Russia. The fastest flight from the region's capital, Vladivostok, to Moscow takes seven hours, while it takes seven days to cross the country by train. When Moscow wakes up, it is already 1 p.m. in Vladivostok! However, information technologies make "virtual migration" possible, allowing workers to communicate in real-time and to study, work, and shop anywhere in the world. A Far Easterner is no longer an aboriginal isolated from the rest of the world; in some cases he or she is even a pacesetter, living in close proximity to digital economy leaders (USA, Japan, South Korea, and China) and to all latest technologies available in the market.

The green economy is another competitive strength for the Russian Far East, with much of its territory being a virgin, uninhabited area. The creation of decent "green" jobs is a global trend that the region may use. This will make the FEFD more attractive for local residents and Russian nationals living in other regions of Russia, but will attract highly-skilled foreign workers, many of whom will see the Russian Far East as a home for them, their children, and grandchildren.

Related Works by the Author

1. Novikova, I. V., Bunina, S. A., & Makarenko, A. S., (2001). Regional aspects of youth employment. *Collected Papers from the Third International Research-to-Practice Conference "Economy, Ecology, and Society of Russia in the 21st Century"* (pp. 649–651). St. Petersburg: SPbSTU.
2. Novikova, I. V., (2002). Problems of the youth labor market in the Amur region. *Papers from the Regional Research-to-Practice Conference of Students, Post-Graduate Students, and Young Researchers of the Amur Region "Future of Amur Science."* Blagoveshchensk: Agrarian Research Center, Far Eastern Branch of the Russian Academy of Science.
3. Novikova, I. V., & Bunina, S. A., (2004). Effects of personnel policy of a city's major employer onto the labor market of the region. *Proceedings of the 1st All-Russian Research-to-Practice Conference "Economical and Social Development of the Regions of Russia"* (pp. 60–62). Penza: RIO PGSHA.
4. Novikova, I. V., & Bunina, S. A., (2004). Problems of youth employment in the region. *Proceedings of the Research-to-Practice Conference "Regional Laws: Experience, Challenges, and Prospects"* (pp. 211–215). Blagoveshchensk: Zeya.
5. Novikova, I. V., (2005). Youth labor market of Amur Region: Trends and prospects. *Collected Papers of the 7th Open Conference: Competition Between Research Papers of Young Scientists of Khabarovsk Territory (Economical Section)* (pp. 127–131). Khabarovsk: RIOTIP.
6. Novikova, I. V., & Bunina, S. A., (2005). Youth labor market model for the region. *Proceedings of the International Research-to-Practice Conference "Support of Young Entrepreneurs and Promotion of Youth Employment"* (pp. 47–50). Penza: RIO PGSHA.
7. Novikova, I. V., Bunina, S. A., & Uvarov, V. A., (2006). *Management of the Youth Labor Market in the Conditions of the Russian Far East.* Khabarovsk: DVAGS.
8. Novikova, I. V., (2006). Management of the regional youth labor market (using Amur Region as an example). *Proceedings of the 8th Open Conference: Competition between Research Papers of Young Scientists of Khabarovsk Territory (Economical Section)* (pp. 138–145). Khabarovsk: RIOTIP.
9. Novikova, I. V., & Bunina, S. A., (2006). Development of the youth labor market in conditions of the Russian Far East. *Proceedings of the Regional Inter-University Research-to-Practice Conference "Higher Education Institutions*

are the Most Important National Resource of Regional Development" (Vol. 1, pp. 11−17). Birobidzhan: Birobidzhan branch of Amur State University.

10. Novikova, I. V., (2011). Youth of Amur Region: Is it the end of the beginning of the path? *From In Search of Russia: A Series of Publications to the Discussion of the Identity Issue* (Vol. 3, pp. 71−82, 313−325). Eastern Russia/Russian Far East, St. Petersburg: Intersocis (in Russian), (in German).

11. Novikova, I. V., (2011). Strategic planning as a form of assistance in employment of students of the universities of Amur Region. *In the World of Scientific Breakthroughs, No. 6.1, 18*, pp. 451−461.

12. Novikova, I. V., & Bezzubko, L. V., (2011). Specifics of strategic planning for development of the Russian regions. *Book of Research Papers of Donetsk State University of Management "Management of Economic Development of Industrial Enterprises"* (pp. 15−19). Ekonomika Series.

13. Novikova, I. V., (2011). Potential for reduction of clandestine employment in the Amur region. *Book of Research Papers of the International Research-to-Practice Conference "Challenging Issues of Science"* (pp. 91−92). RF Ministry of Education and Science. Tambov: TROO "Biznes-Nauka-Obshchestvo, Part 1.

14. Novikova, I. V., (2011). Forecast of supply and demand dynamics of the labor market in the Amur region. *In the World of Scientific Breakthroughs, No. 10.1*, pp. 536−549.

15. Novikova, I. V., Kutaev, S. K., & Vishnevskaya, N. G., (2013). *Conceptual Basis of Functioning and Development of the Labor Market: Regional Experience.* Moscow: Pero.

16. Novikova, I. V., (2013). Development of entrepreneurship in trade as a factor of easing tension in the labor market of Amur Region. *Proceedings of the International Research-to-Practice Conference The 5th Naidenov's Readings "Business Developments in Trade and Services: Problems and Prospects"* (pp. 36−38). Moscow: Nauchnaya Biblioteka.

17. Novikova, I. V., (2013). Migration processes in the Amur region as a factor of formation of the regional labor market. *Proceedings of the International Research-to-Practice Conference "Topical Issues of Modern Economy in the Global World"* (pp. 260−264). Makhachkala: DGU.

18. Novikova, I. V., & Leskina, O. N., (2013). Areas of concern of regional labor markets (comparative analysis of Amur Region and Penza Region). *In the World of Scientific Breakthroughs, 8*(44), 166−178.

19. Novikova, I. V., & Koroleva, S. I., (2014). Labor market of Amur Region: Labor force deficit grows! *Issues of Business and Economics* (Vol. 2, pp. 5−10). Vestnik Akademii.

20. Novikova, I. V., (2014). Assistance to formation of labor resources in development programs of for territories of the Russian Far East. *All-Russian Research Journal Mikroekonomika, 4*, 88−92.

21. Novikova, I. V., & Tryukhan, T. A., (2014). Far Eastern guarantees of the State as the source of growth of the Gross Regional Product. *In the World of Scientific Breakthroughs* (Vol. 5.2, No. 53, pp. 812−820). Sotsialno-Gumanitarnye Nauki.

22. Novikova, I. V., (2014). Clandestine employment as a constituent of economy of Far Eastern Federal District. *Business Education Law, Herald of Volgograd Institute of Business, 3*(28), 183−186.

23. Novikova, I. V., & Tryukhan, T. A., (2014). Role of the employed in formation of gross regional product of far Eastern Federal District. *Business Education Law, Herald of Volgograd Institute of Business, 3*(28), 124−127.

24. Novikova, I. V., (2014). Attraction of compatriots residing abroad as a method to solve the problem of the deficit labor market, *Proceedings of the International Research-to-Practice Conference "Topical Issues of the Modern Economy in the Global World"* (pp. 214−217). Makhachkala: DGU.

25. Novikova, I. V., (2014). Effect of migration onto labor market of Amur Region. *Proceedings of the International Research-to-Practice Conference, The 6th Naidenov's Readings, "Business Developments in Trade and Services: Problems and Prospects"* (pp. 295−296). Moscow: Nauchnaya Biblioteka.

26. Novikova, I. V., & Tsapko, Y. E., (2015). Problems and prospects of labor market development in the Far Eastern Federal District. *All-Russian Research Journal Mikroekonomika, 1*, 117−121.

27. Novikova, I. V., (2015). Who lives well in Russia? (Or thinking about living costs in the Russian Far East). *Proceedings of the International Research-to-Practice Conference, The 6th Naidenov's Readings, "Business Developments in Trade and Services: Problems and Prospects* (pp. 215−24)." Moscow: Nauchnaya Biblioteka.

28. Novikova, I. V., (2015). Far Eastern guarantees as an instrument for development of the territory. *Issues of Business and Economics, Herald of the Academy of Science, 1*, 59−63.

29. Novikova, I. V., (2016). *Regulation of Employment in the Russian Far East.* Lambert.

30. Novikova, I. V., (2016). Prospects of using the Far Eastern governmental guarantees as an instrument for promotion of employment in the region. *Living Standards in Regions of Russia, 1*, 206−219.

31. Novikova, I. V., (2016). Human resourcing of programs of development of the Russian Far East. *Proceedings of the 8th International Research-to-Practice Conference "From Recession to Stabilization and Economic Upturn"* (pp. 156−166). Moscow: FGBOU VO Plekhanov's Russian University of Economics.

32. Novikova, I. V., (2016). Breakthrough growth of labor force quality is the basis for advanced development of the Russian Far East. In: Margania, S. A., Belozerov, et al., (eds.), *Proceedings of the 3rd International Research-to-Practice Conference "Sustainable Development: Society and Economy"* (p. 381). Editorial Board: O. L. St. Petersburg: SpGU Skifia-Print.

33. Novikova, I. V., (2016). Model for regulation of employment in the Far Eastern Federal District. In: Grebennikov, V. G., & Shchepina, I. N., (eds.), *System Simulation of Socioeconomic Processes: Papers of the 39th International Research Workshop-School, St. Petersburg* (pp. 339−342). Voronezh: Voronezh State Pedagogical University.

34. Novikova, I. V., (2016). Labor of the far easterners may turn a profit for business. *Proceedings of the 3ʳᵈ Virtual International Research-to-Practice Conference "Innovative Development of Contemporary Socioeconomic Systems"* (pp. 333–337). The RF Ministry of Education and Science, FGBOU VO Komsomolsk-on-Amur State Technical University, FAO Dalnii of the Market under the RF Ministry of Regional Development.

35. Novikova, I. V., (2017). Information potential of employment sector is a new factor for stabilization of demographic situation in the Russian Far East. *Living Standards of Regions of Russia, 2,* 135–142.

36. Novikova, I. V., (2017). Government regulation of employment in the terms of assistance to formation of labor force capacity of the Russian Far East. *Book of Papers of the International Research-to-Practice Conference "State Management and Development of Russia: Models and Projects* (Vol. 2, pp. 607–614). Moscow: Prospekt (RANEPA).

37. Novikova, I. V., (2017). Noospheric humanology as the basis of innovation development of the Russian Far East. In: Imanov, G. M., & Gorbunov, A. A., (eds.), *Noospherism is a New Path of Development* (Vol. 2, pp. 835–842). St. Petersburg: Asterion.

38. Novikova, I. V., (2017). *Regulation of Employment in the Russian Far East.* Moscow: Ruscience.

39. Novikova, I. V., (2017). Strategic employee exchange and voucher employment as the means to reduce precarious employment in the region. In: Valentey, S. D., (ed.), *"What Human Resources Does the Russian Economy Need?:" Proceedings from the 7ᵗʰ International Research-to-Practice Conference "Readings from Abalkin"* (pp. 163–173). Moscow: FGBOU VO Plekhanov's Russian University of Economics.

40. Novikova, I. V., Loktyukhina, N. V., & Zabelina, O. V., (2018). Regulation of employment in the Russian Far East. *Economy and Management: Problems and Solutions, 4*(1/73), 3–12.

41. Novikova, I. V., (2018). Contemporary role of Far Eastern guarantees in earnings of local population and directions of upgrading their use. *Incomes, Expenses, and Savings of the RF population: Trends and Prospects, Proceedings of the 3ʳᵈ International Research-to-Practice Conference* (pp. 68–71). ISEPN RAS. Moscow: Fabrika Ofsetnoy Pechati LLC.

42. Novikova I.V., Yao L. (2020). China-Russia Strategic Cooperation in Labour Development. *Administrative Consulting, 5,* 60–67. https://doi.org/10.22394/1726-1139-2020-5-60-67.

43. Novikova I.V. (2019). The development of a system of "green" skills in the strategizing of labor resources of industrial enterprises. *Russian Journal of Industrial Economics, 12*(4), 484–493. https://doi.org/10.17073/2072-1633-2019-4-484-493.

44. Novikova I.V. (2019). Strategic enterprise resource management in Industry 4.0. *The Economic Revival of Russia, 3,* 181–184.

Index